INTRODUCING FREEMASONRY

INTRODUCING FREEMASONRY

A Practical Guide to Masonic Practice in England and Wales

M. de Pace

Ian Allan Group

LONDON

LEWIS MASONIC

Published by
LEWIS MASONIC, Terminal House, Shepperton
Members of the IAN ALLAN GROUP

ISBN 0 85318 133 0

First published in the United Kingdom in 1983

British Library Cataloguing in Publication Data
De Pace, M.
Introducing freemasonry.
1. Freemasons
I. Title
366'.1 HS395
ISBN 0-85318-133-0

Made and printed in Great Britain by
The Garden City Press Limited
Letchworth, Hertfordshire SG6 1JS

FOREWORD

I wholeheartedly recommend this book not only to young or "new" Masons but also to all brethren who are interested in finding out how our vast organisation ticks. The book tells us in detailed and uncomplicated language how the system works, starting with individual Lodges and its Officers and progressing through to Provinces and Grand Lodge.

In it we can learn about the origin and aims of our great Charities, which are currently undergoing rationalisation in the light of the *Bagnall Report*, and I regard *Introducing Freemasonry* as one of the best and most comprehensive reference books on the Craft which is available to us all.

September 1983 Guy Halsey, TD, JP

PROVINCIAL GRAND MASTER OF HERTFORDSHIRE

PREFACE

THIS IS A book for young Masons written by a young Mason. The word "young" refers, of course, to length of membership not age. The author hopes that being a young Mason still, gives him a perspective on the needs of other young Masons which more experienced members of the Craft may no longer have.

The world of Masonry is an exciting and stimulating one to the new member and he is naturally curious about it. He encounters traditions, expressions, and structures, all of which are strange to him, and then looks for a ready source of information which will answer his many questions. There are many books for him to read, but few which deal in introductory form with the structure of the society to which he has been admitted a member.

He finds it difficult to get a clear picture of the system of rank by which recognition is given for Masonic service, or to appreciate the framework which will enable him to perceive where he stands in relation to the rest of the Craft or, for that matter, to the other Masonic orders. He would like to know more about the Masonic Charities, or about what happens at Grand Lodge. It is to these, and many other questions of a practical nature, that this book is addressed.

It will be appreciated, however, that by focusing on practical matters, where wide variation exists from one Province to another and even from one Lodge to another, some of the details given will not apply in all cases. In dealing with matters such as the proceedings at Masonic Dinners, Lodge work, or Provincial custom, the information contained in this book is intended to serve as a general guide rather than a description of established practice. Nor is separate attention given to Districts in respect of their organisation and government. Their systems are not identical to those of the Provinces but are sufficiently similar to make continual distinction a distraction in what is essentially a basic introduction to Masonic practice in England and Wales.

ABOUT THE AUTHOR

BRO DE PACE was born in South Africa where he spent his early years. He graduated in Philosophy and Psychology at the University of Pretoria, and then came to London. He is employed by a City of London firm, where he is responsible for the introduction of new systems and technology. He has always had a strong interest in the structure of organisations, and derives great enjoyment from the process of discovering how the various parts fit together. He was Initiated in 1979, and found himself fascinated by Freemasonry: not only by its moral teachings (which have had a salutary effect on him), but by its existence as a complex organisation which in this country has over half a million members.

CONTENTS

APPENDIX

PROGRESSION

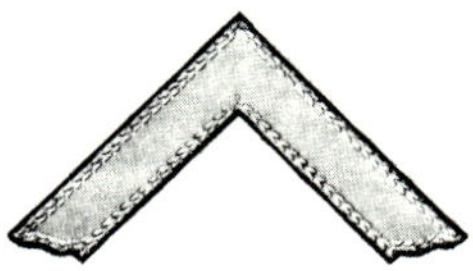

INTRODUCTION

The regular Officers of a Lodge are the Master, his two Wardens, a Treasurer, a Secretary, two Deacons, an Inner Guard, and a Tyler. All other Officers are additional, and Lodges may employ all or some of these according to their individual traditions.

For present purposes a full complement of additional Officers is assumed, and the offices of a Lodge are divided into two groups: those leading to the chair of Worshipful Master, and those usually (though not always) held by Past Masters.

TO THE CHAIR

The sequence of offices leading to that of Worshipful Master is usually as follows:

Steward
Inner Guard
Junior Deacon
Senior Deacon
Junior Warden
Senior Warden
Worshipful Master

The Worshipful Master is elected at the Lodge meeting preceding that of Installation. The qualification for the office of Worshipful Master is one year's service as Senior or Junior Warden. While it is customary for the Senior Warden to be elected to the chair of Master, the procedure of election ensures that it is not automatic but at the discretion of the members of the Lodge.

Progression is usually based upon seniority but ultimately it rests with the Master to appoint his Officers, which he does at the Installation meeting having previously received their agreement. In practice, commitments at work or other reasons may prevent someone from finding the time to prepare for the next office. In such cases the gap may be filled by a Past Master, by moving the entire line up an extra position, or by inviting a capable brother from a lower office to jump a few offices.

Lodges vary in the expectation they place upon the incumbent Master as regards the work he has to perform at meetings, but each prospective Master needs to determine at an early date a schedule of the work to be learnt. The following gives an indication of the work a Master might be expected to perform during his year in office:

Appointing and Investing his Officers
Closing the Lodge
Chairing the Dinner (Festive Board)
Opening the Lodge
Initiation Ceremony
Charge to the Initiate
Passing Ceremony
Explanation of the Second Degree Tracing Board
Raising Ceremony
Traditional History, Third Degree Tracing Board and Working Tools
Installing his successor

This list represents *Emulation* work. Other workings or individual Lodge traditions may dictate a different content. For example, the Explanation of the Second Degree Tracing Board will rarely be found in *Stability* working. It is also worth bearing in mind that the sequence of work, other than that of the three degrees, will be as laid out above.

In the year following, as Immediate Past Master and seated to the immediate left of his successor, he will be responsible for supporting the Worshipful Master during the meeting and, if so dictated by Lodge tradition, at the dinner. Should the Master be unable to attend a meeting, the Immediate Past Master will take his chair at the meeting and dinner.

While the amount of work seems daunting, in practice it is not, for it has been mastered by hundreds of thousands, each of whom began with no prior experience of committing large sections of text to memory, and most with no more than average abilities. Consider that in 1950 the number 7,000 was reached on the Register of the United Grand Lodge of England and Wales, giving approximately 6,000 active Lodges. If these 6,000 Lodges were active during the thirty years up to 1980, they would have installed 180,000 Masters during that short period alone.

OFFICERS

The Officers of a Lodge, other than those leading to the Chair, and ranked in order of seniority, are:

Chaplain
Treasurer
Secretary
Director of Ceremonies
Charity Steward
Almoner
Assistant Director of Ceremonies
Organist
Assistant Secretary
Tyler

These offices are usually filled by Past Masters. The office of Organist, since it requires a special skill which may not be present among the Lodge membership, may remain vacant with its duties being carried out by a member of another Lodge. The Tyler often performs his office for a number of Lodges. In such cases, a small fee (which could include free entry to the dinner) will usually be paid for their services. Alternatively, either or both could be subscribing members of the Lodge, appointed by the Master.

Of the above, only the Treasurer and Tyler (the latter if not appointed) are elected by the members of the Lodge; the remainder are appointed by the Master for the year. During his brief spell as Master Elect, he will have approached his intended Officers and obtained their agreement to take or continue in office. While the appointment of these Officers is at the sole discretion of the Master, in practice he often makes no changes at all, allowing the incumbents to remain in their offices should they so desire. An incumbent may remain in office for many years because of his particular suitability to the job, or simply because no one is inclined to ask him to stand down. Most changes in office occur through the incumbents themselves offering to stand down in favour of those who have not held office. Consideration may, for example, be given to the prospect of Provincial honours for a younger member of the Lodge. A majority consensus of opinion may, at times, persuade Officers to 'retire' but there are many instances where sensitivity to the feelings of the person in question ensures that he never becomes aware of such an opinion. There are, too, occasions when a determined Master will ring the changes without waiting for volunteers. However, unless he is supported by a substantial body of opinion, and even then, it is a risky undertaking which could divide a Lodge, or worse, have as consequence a member who feels rejected by and alienated from his Lodge.

The Offices

The office of Chaplain is, not surprisingly, a devotional one. He offers the prayers of the Lodge but need not be a man of the cloth.

The Treasurer is responsible for the receipt and banking of funds, making payments, and the maintenance of a set of accounts. He also prepares an annual statement of account for auditing and circulation to the members of the Lodge, and provides the financial control over the Lodge income and expenditure.

The Secretary keeps the Lodge minutes and is responsible for the general paperwork including the issue of summonses, the annual returns to Grand Lodge, liaison with Provincial Grand Lodge, dealings with other Lodges, and communications from and to members. He is expected to have a sound knowledge of the regulations of the Craft, and may well be consulted by the Master on points of procedure.

The Director of Ceremonies is responsible for the smooth running of the meeting. He should ensure that all articles necessary for a meeting are laid out correctly, arrange processions into and from the Lodge, receive important visitors and attend to matters of protocol such as the salutes to Grand Officers.

The Charity Steward is basically a fund-raiser. He collects donations, explains the advantages of covenants, and disseminates information about the various Charities and their work to ensure that all members appreciate the use to which their donations are put, and to encourage them to be as generous as their personal circumstances permit.

The Almoner keeps in touch with members and their families at times of illness or in old age. Lodge funds may be allocated for use by the Almoner for specific purposes such as the distribution of Christmas cards and gifts to widows. Each Almoner has his own methods, but typically an Almoner would arrange visits to those in hospital, organise practical help for members when they or their families are in difficulties, or simply visit members who find themselves unable to attend meetings.

The other offices, except for that of Tyler which is discussed elsewhere, need no further elaboration.

PROVINCIAL HONOURS

A Provincial Grand Master is empowered to appoint each year a number of acting Provincial Grand Officers, the maximum number being determined on a sliding scale according to the number of Lodges in the Province. Thus, a Province of 60 to 79 Lodges may have 28 acting Officers, while a larger Province of 200 to 219 Lodges may have 49. The additional Officers in the larger Provinces are mainly related to the needs of larger Provincial meetings, eg more Deacons, Deputy and Assistant Directors of Ceremonies, Stewards, etc. Rule 68(a) in the *Book of Constitutions* contains a schedule of the Officers that may be appointed depending on the number of Lodges in the Province. This rule is changed from time to time: the figures given above are taken from the 1979 edition.

The holders of most of the offices change from year to

year, while others, particularly those who provide continuity such as the Provincial Grand Secretary, remain in office for several years. Note, however, that in most Provinces, with the exception of those continuing in office, an Officer seen at work at a Provincial Grand Lodge meeting will generally have been appointed at the previous meeting. After a year in office such an Officer will retain his rank as a past Officer.

A Provincial Grand Master is further empowered to make appointments to past Provincial Grand Office. These past ranks are on par with rank retained by previously acting Officers. The number of Officers appointed each year, acting and past, is limited to four for every five Lodges in the Province. In addition, one appointment to past rank may be made for every reappointment, ie where, say, the Provincial Grand Director of Ceremonies continues in office.

Provincial honours are bestowed mainly on Past Masters, but the award of a Provincial honour is not automatic, nor does it always follow after a set period from the date of installation as Master: it is awarded on merit. Many Provinces do follow the practice of awarding Provincial rank after a set period, which varies from six years to eleven years depending on the Province, but it is never a hard and fast rule. Other Provinces do not observe any conditions of time when conferring Provincial rank. In all cases, the Provincial Grand Master has absolute discretion in awarding Provincial rank.

Past Masters are not the only recipients of Provincial rank. It may also be conferred on those who have given good service but are unlikely to attain the position of Master. In the Province of Cumberland and Westmorland, for example, the rank of Provincial Grand Steward is conferred on such members.

Due to the limit on the number of Officers that may be appointed each year, a system of selection is necessary. In some Provinces, each Lodge Secretary is responsible for completing and forwarding to Provincial Grand Lodge a form of recommendation containing information about the

Lodge candidate. Such information includes details of ceremonies he has conducted, offices held in the Lodge, attendance at Lodge, and other information regarding the service he has given to his Lodge. In other Provinces written reports are compiled by the Provincial Grand Master or his representatives following visits to Lodges. These reports have particular reference to the work of the Master and the Past Masters. In a small Province, such as Cambridgeshire, formal reports are unnecessary since the prospective candidates are well known to the senior Officers of the Province. Another method is that followed by West Lancashire, a large Province of well over 500 Lodges, which is split into Groups on geographical lines. The Lodges in a particular area are formed into a Group and a Group Chairman (usually a Grand Officer) is responsible for making recommendations for Provincial Rank.

Some Provincial Grand Officers may subsequently become eligible for further Provincial honours in the form of promotion to a higher rank. Promotion is given in recognition of merit and continued service to the Lodge and the Province. No general timescale applies although some Provinces allow a minimum number of years such as seven or ten to elapse before giving consideration to promotion. However, since promotion is based on merit, the ability of and the work done by an Officer may result in early promotion. Another factor which influences both the first appointment to Provincial Rank, and subsequent promotion, is the need to ensure fair distribution of Provincial honours among the various Lodges or give recognition on behalf of a Lodge. In some Provinces certain past ranks are reserved for those receiving promotion. For example, the rank of Past Provincial Senior Warden may be considered prestigious and only awarded where particular recognition is required.

The rank of Provincial Grand Steward is variously interpreted. In several Provinces, Provincial Grand Stewards are automatically recommended for promotion following their year of office (without necessarily receiving promotion:

again good service during the period of office is a prerequisite). In Somerset, for example, the promotion is usually to Provincial Grand Deacon. In Dorset, where Provincial Grand Stewards accompany and escort the Provincial Grand Master or his Deputy or Assistant to all Installation meetings, they are appointed the year following their year in the Chair, and then promoted after seven years to a past rank. In the Eastern Division of South Wales, Provincial Grand Stewards are considered an extension of the Provincial Executive: a red apron will be found in most Lodges since they retain their ranks for at least five years before they are promoted.

The rank of a Provincial Grand Officer, whether acting or past, may be determined from the emblem of office shown on the jewel and apron. The latter has dark blue edging, except for Provincial Grand Stewards, acting or past, who have crimson edging to their aprons. Seniority and identification is given below. Note however that a Provincial Grand Master and his deputy and assistant(s) wear chains of office when officially present at a Lodge in his Province, and Provincial Grand Stewards are more easily identified by their crimson regalia.

1. Prov G Master	:	*Compasses and square with five pointed star*
2. Deputy Prov G Master	:	*Square*
3. Assistant Prov G Master	:	*Inverted square with word* Assistant *added*
4. Prov Senior G Warden	:	*Level*
5. Prov Junior G Warden	:	*Plumb rule*
6. Prov G Chaplain	:	*Open Book on triangle and glory*
7. Prov G Treasurer	:	*Key*
8. Prov G Registrar	:	*Scroll with seal*
9. Prov G Secretary	:	*Two quill pens in saltire, tied by a ribbon*

10. Prov G Director of Ceremonies	:	*Two rods in saltire, tied by a ribbon*
11. Prov G Sword Bearer	:	*Two swords in saltire with a ribbon*
12. Prov G Superintendent of Works	:	*Semicircular protractor*
13. Prov Deputy G Chaplain	:	*As 6 above with word* Deputy *added*
14. Deputies to 8 to 12 above following their rank	:	*As 8 to 12 above with word* Deputy *added*
15. Prov Senior G Deacon	:	*Dove and olive branch*
16. Prov Junior G Deacon	:	*Dove and olive branch*
17. Prov Asst G Chaplain	:	*As 6 above with word* Assistant *added*
18. Assistants to 8 to 12 above following their rank	:	*As 8 to 12 above with word* Assistant *added*
19. Prov G Organist	:	*Lyre*
20. Prov G Standard Bearer	:	*Two banners, staves in saltire, tied by a ribbon*
21. Prov Asst G Std Bearer	:	*As above with word* Assistant *added*
22. Prov Deputy G Organist	:	*Lyre with word* Deputy *added*
23. Prov G Pursuivant	:	*Grand Lodge coat of arms on crossed sword and rod*
24. Prov Asst G Pursuivant	:	*As above with word* Assistant *added*
25. Prov G Steward	:	*Cornucopia*
26. Prov G Tyler	:	*Vertical sword*

The offices of Provincial Deputy Grand Sword Bearer, Provincial Deputy Grand Superintendent of Works, and Provincial Deputy Grand Organist will be found only in the largest Provinces.

Acting Provincial Grand Officers are distinguished from Past Provincial Grand Officers by the shape and colour of their jewel which is round and unadorned for the former; oval with a blue enamelled background for the latter.

Illustrations of all jewels and emblems will be found in the *Book of Constitutions* available from the Enquiries Office, Freemasons' Hall.

DISTRICT GRAND LODGES

Lodges meeting outside the United Kingdom are formed into Districts and function in a similar way to Provincial Grand Lodges in England and Wales. District honours are appointed in a similar manner to Provincial honours.

LONDON GRAND RANK

London Grand Rank is the equivalent of Provincial honours for members of London Lodges. The latter have no central government other than Grand Lodge itself. London Lodges are today defined as those which are held within five miles of Freemasons' Hall (until 1971 it had been 10 miles). London Grand Rank is conferred on Past Masters of London Lodges by the Grand Master to a number each year not exceeding one for every two such Lodges.

It differs from Provincial Grand Rank in that there are no offices to be filled, being purely of an honorary nature. It is the equivalent of past office in a Province, but since there are no offices and thus no grading by precedence of office, all are at the same level. Another difference is that only Past Masters are eligible, and then only five years after installing a successor. Details similar to that supplied in a Province, are provided of each candidate.

A recently introduced second tier of seniority is that of Senior London Grand Rank, which is a promotion from

London Grand Rank. The jewel and apron of Senior London Grand Rank shows a square, level and plumb rule while those of London Grand Rank show the Past Master's emblem of Square and 47th proposition of the First Book of Euclid.

OVERSEAS GRAND RANK

This is conferred on Past Masters of Lodges outside of the United Kingdom and who are not controlled by a District Grand Lodge.

GRAND RANK

The appointment of Grand Officers and the conferment of Past Grand rank is the prerogative of the Grand Master. In practice he is assisted and advised by a Council which has no formal status but nevertheless exists to ease the task of judging and selecting from amongst those who have been proposed.

In London, each Lodge selects a suitably qualified person as candidate and puts his name forward for Grand honours. Selection may not be immediate, and names may be withdrawn in favour of an alternative if a delay occurs since only one candidate may be proposed by a Lodge at any one time. In the Province, it is the Provincial Grand Master who is invited to submit candidates for Grand Rank.

The number of Grand Officers that may be appointed each year is defined in the *Book of Constitutions*. Including the permanent positions they number just under 80. Also included in this number are the 19 Grand Stewards permitted by the *Constitutions*. There are, in addition, 86 Provincial Grand Masters, District Grand Masters, and Grand Inspectors (the latter to govern groups of Lodges overseas but not under a District).

The Grand Master may each year also make appointments (or promotions) to past Grand rank. Typically, in the region of 300 such appointments are made in a year. These represent the 8,000 plus Lodges under the Constitution of the United Grand Lodge. In total there are approximately 5,000 Grand Officers holding past rank.

Grand Officers are identified by the sprig of acacia and ear of corn emblems on their aprons, jewels, and collars. The seniority is much as in Provincial Grand Lodge except that Provincial and District Grand Masters rank above the Senior Grand Warden, and certain other appointments are unique to Grand Lodge such as the President of the Board of General Purposes whose office ranks after Grand Chaplain, and the Presidents of the Grand Charity and Masonic Foundation for the Aged and the Sick, which offices rank after the Grand Secretary.

'HIGHER' DEGREES

'HIGHER' DEGREES

The degrees outside Craft Freemasonry are higher in one sense only: they require at least Craft Master Mason status as entrance qualification.

The preferred expressions are 'side degrees' or 'additional degrees'. Had one of those forms been used here, there would, of course, have been no need for the quotation marks surrounding the word 'higher'. However, the emphasis of this book is on the practical, hence the use of the colloquial form 'higher degrees'.

Some require, in addition, membership of one or more other Orders such as the Royal Arch or Mark. They do not, however, represent stages of progression beyond Craft Freemasonry, which consists only of the three degrees and the Installation ceremony. The notion that there is some grand Masonic scheme in which one progresses to the highest degree, and in which the Craft degrees represent the lowest steps, has no substance. All other degrees belong to Masonic Orders which are independent, each having its own government, organisation and means of according recognition to members who have given good service.

The Order which is closest to the Craft is that of the Royal Arch. Its degree was once worked as a fourth degree and at the constitution of the United Grand Lodge, the Royal Arch was given recognition together with the regular three Craft degrees.

Part of the 2nd Article of the Act of Union in 1813 is still reproduced in every copy of the *Book of Constitutions*, ie it was 'declared and pronounced that pure Antient Masonry consists of three degrees and no more, viz those of the Entered Apprentice, the Fellow Craft, and the Master Mason, including the Supreme Order of the Holy Royal Arch'. In this sense the Royal Arch is not a 'higher' degree. It is, however, regulated by a separate Order and requires separate admission and membership, neither of which follows, as a matter of course, from Craft membership. In practical terms, therefore, it is a degree outside Craft Masonry.

In content the Royal Arch degree is equally close to the Craft: it continues the Masonic theme of Craft Freemasonry, developing it to its inescapable conclusion.

Even so, the proportion of members of the Craft entering the Royal Arch is no more than a third. Some masons join several Orders in an attempt to quench their thirst for more Masonry; others are put off by the thought of the extra work involved or the additional cost. It is necessary, however, to bear in mind that there is often a long waiting list for office in other Orders, as well as a requirement for the qualification of Past Master in the Craft for certain offices. The work, when it comes, may be at a stage when the preparations towards and for the Chair in the Craft is in the past.

Another point to consider is that the amount of work varies from Order to Order, and depending on the stage one has reached in one's Masonic career, the work of one Order may be easier to accommodate than that of another. It is possible, by judicious selection, to plan a Masonic career which will provide extra enjoyment without necessarily imposing too heavy a load in respect of work. Equally, it is possible to select memberships which will not impose too great a financial burden. A price list showing the cost of regalia is obtainable from regalia suppliers such as Toye, Kenning & Spencer or Lewis Masonic (see under Booksellers in the section on Education). The cost of admission is usually quite low by comparison with, say, the annual subscription, while the size of the latter depends on dining costs in the geographic area and on the standard of dining set by the individual Chapter, etc. The Secretary, Registrar, Recorder, or Scribe E (depending on the Order) will be only too happy to furnish enquirers with details of the costs involved. The names, addresses and telephone numbers of such officers are available in Year Books issued by the Provinces.

Another factor, outside the scope of this book, but one

which may influence the choice of Order or Orders is the content of their degrees and the lessons they teach. While such information is not always communicated to a prospective candidate, it is available, if only in books, and may for some be an over-riding consideration, particularly where a degree of another Order links in with or extends a degree with which they may already be familiar.

Finally, admission to other Masonic Orders is not available on demand: it is by invitation. But it is unlikely that interest shown in a specific Order will be ignored by its members. They, having benefited from their membership of the Order, will enjoy the opportunity of extending its benefits to another.

ROYAL ARCH

The Royal Arch ceremony deals with the rediscovery of the secrets which were lost by the death of Hiram Abif. It also sets out to communicate the concept of God and provides a fitting conclusion to the spiritual journey begun in Craft Freemasonry.

The Royal Arch is the only Masonic Order which is officially recognised by the United Grand Lodge of England and Wales. Indeed the Grand Lodge *Constitutions* and the General Regulations of Royal Arch Masonry are bound together and published in a single book. The only non-Craft jewel which is permitted in a Craft Lodge is that of the Royal Arch.

This situation came about as one result of the Union of the two rival Grand Lodges in 1813. The 'Antients' had practiced the Royal Arch as a fourth degree, and contained in one of the Articles of Union was an item to the effect that the Supreme Order of the Holy Royal Arch was considered a part of 'pure Antient Masonry'.

Every Royal Arch Chapter is attached to a regular Lodge, taking on the number and precedence of the Lodge to which it is attached. Chapters may be transferred from one Lodge to another (changing its name and number in the process), but no more than one Chapter may be attached to a Lodge at any one time.

Qualifications

It is necessary to have been a Master Mason for at least four weeks to qualify for admission to the Order. However, it is not possible to be elected as a Principal unless one has previously been installed as Master of a Lodge.

Progression

The sequence of Offices leading to that of First Principal is as follows:

Steward
Second Assistant Sojourner
First Assistant Sojourner
Principal Sojourner
Scribe Nehemiah
Joshua (Third Principal)
Haggai (Second Principal)
Zerubbabel (First Principal)

Qualifications, other than that already given, for offices are:

Third Principal	:	A full year's service in the Office of Scribe Ezra or Nehemia, Principal Sojourner or Assistant Sojourner.
Second Principal	:	A full year's service in the Office of Third Principal.
First Principal	:	A full year's service in the Office of Second Principal.

A First Principal may not hold his Office for more than three years in succession, a Second Principal for more than two years.

The Work
There is only one degree: the ceremony of Exaltation ie the acceptance of a new member. The work is given below. To convey the extent of each Officer's work, comparisons are made with equivalent work in the Craft. Where no equivalent exists, the Charge to the Initiate is used as a measure, for length if not for style.

> The First Principal conducts the ceremony. His work in this respect is just over half that of the Master in the first degree not counting the Charge to the Initiate.
> The Principal Sojourner, who has a role partly equivalent to that of Deacon, has a contribution which, in length, is slightly greater than that of the Charge to the Initiate.
> The Scribe Nehemiah has a role equivalent to that of Inner Guard with a slightly greater contribution.
> The Third Principal gives a lecture just over half the length of the Charge to the Initiate.
> The Second Principal gives a lecture which, in length, is slightly greater than that of the Charge to the Initiate.
> The First Principal gives a lecture which is approximately twice the length of the Charge to the Initiate.

During the Installation Ceremony, each Principal installs his successor.

There are many different published workings including *Domatic, Aldersgate, Complete, Taylor's*, and several others. As in the Craft, there is no injunction to use a specific ritual.

Cost

The cost of the regalia for a Companion is approximately twice that of the Master Mason apron. The fee for exaltation is usually quite small. The current fee together with the cost of the annual subscription may be obtained from the Treasurer or Scribe E of a local Royal Arch Chapter.

Regalia

Description: The regalia consists of an apron, sash and jewel. The apron is white with a border of indented crimson and dark blue. It has two gilt tassels suspended from ribbons and a triangular overlap. The sash, also of crimson and dark blue, is worn over the left shoulder. The jewel, consisting of two interlaced triangles within a double circle, is suspended from a ribbon worn on the left breast. A Triple Tau within a triangle appears on the apron overlap and at the point of the sash.

Rank: Some, but by no means all, of the regalia differences are given below to enable a Companion to identify the various ranks which are likely to be seen at a meeting of a private Chapter.

Companions are identified by white ribbons from which the jewel and tassels are suspended, and a white background to the Triple Taus on the apron and sash.

Chapter Officers wear a crimson collar from which is suspended the jewel of their office.

Principals, present and past, are identified by crimson ribbons and a crimson background to the Triple Taus. Past First Principals wear a crimson collar with a gilt braid running down the centre.

Provincial Officers and Holders of London Grand Chapter Rank wear a tri-coloured jewel ribbon (dark blue, crimson, and light blue) and have a dark blue background to the Triple Taus. The emblem of office is shown on the apron contained within a double circle. Present Officers are distinguished from past Officers by the size of the jewel of office (three inch diameter for the former, two inch diameter for the latter) which is suspended from a tri-colour collar. The jewel of office of a Grand Superintendent, the Provincial head, is suspended from a chain of gold or gilt.

Grand Officers are identified by a double border on the apron. The emblem of office on the apron is contained within two branches of laurel in gilt.

Since the Royal Arch jewel may be worn at meetings of Craft Lodges, the ribbon differences of Royal Arch rank may also be observed at Craft meetings.

Governing Body

The Supreme Grand Chapter of Royal Arch Masons of England is based in Great Queen Street at Freemasons' Hall. It employs an organisation similar to that of the United Grand Lodge in having Provincial and District Grand Chapters, each under a Grand Superintendent who has jurisdiction within his area. Provincial and District meetings are held as in the Craft, and both present and past Officers may be appointed. The number of such Officers that may be appointed is according to the number of Chapters in the Province or District. One past rank may be conferred each year for every three Chapters provided that there are at least 21 Chapters in the Province or District. Similar appointments may be made in London by conferring London Grand Chapter Rank. Such Companions may subsequently be promoted to Senior London Grand Chapter Rank.

As in the Craft, administrative and financial control is carried out through a General Purposes Committee.

Historical Background

It is not certain how or when the Royal Arch Ceremony started. The indications are that following the introduction of speculative Masonry to France, social and/or religious factors led French Masons to develop extra degrees.

The Royal Arch degree may have been worked in this country before the middle of the eighteenth century, but there is little evidence until the 1760s. We do know that it was regarded as a fourth degree by the Antients who controlled the use of the degree from within their Grand Lodge up to 1813 when the two Grand Lodges formed a Union. The premier Grand Lodge would have no part of the Royal Arch within their constitution, and an independent body, the Grand and Royal Chapter of Jerusalem was constituted in London in 1766 by Lord Blayney who was at the time also the Grand Master of the premier Grand Lodge. Following the Union of the two Grand Lodges in 1813, matters drifted until 1817 when the body that later became known as the Supreme Grand Chapter was born, recognised and acknowledged by the United Grand Lodge, and representing all Royal Arch interests in England.

The Royal Arch ritual developed throughout the second half of the eighteenth century, the major changes taking place in that part of the ritual which is today taken up with the Lectures. During this period the Lectures were in the form of catechisms. In 1833–34 it was determined by Supreme Grand Chapter to appoint a committee to revise the ritual. The revisions were particularly concerned with the Installation of the Principals, but also affected the duties of the Principal Sojourner and the lectures given by the First and Second Principals. It was probably at this point that the narrative form of the lectures became the standard usage. The revised ceremony was confirmed by 1836, and ordered to be adopted by every Chapter. This is the ceremony which, with minor variations, is worked today.

Further Reading:

1. *Freemasons' Book of the Royal Arch* by Bernard E. Jones. This book is particularly useful to those interested in tracing the origins and growth of the Order.
2. *Freemasons' Royal Arch Guide* by E. E. Ogilvie. The author covers in detail the duties of the Officers, together with biblical histories of the characters, and explanations of the Triple Tau and other emblems. The discussions are based on *Aldersgate* working, a point to be kept in mind by readers who use other workings.
3. There are several papers in the Transactions of the Quatuor Coronati Lodge which are well worth consulting. The Concise Index, available from the Secretary, provides a list of these papers (up to volume 80) together with references to the volumes which contain them.

KNIGHT TEMPLAR

The United, Religious and Masonic Orders of the Temple and of St John of Jerusalem, Palestine, Rhodes and Malta (referred to as Great Priory), govern the Knight Templar degree, and those of the Order of Malta.

There are two Orders: the Knight Templar degree is conferred under the Order of the Temple, while the Order of Malta confers the Knight of St Paul and the Knight of Malta degrees. The Knight of the Temple degree is conferred by Preceptories, ie the Meetings of Knights Templar. The degrees of Knight of St Paul and Knight of Malta can be worked by Priories, but is usually worked at meetings of the Provincial Priory. At such meetings the degrees of the Order of Malta are conferred on all those in the Province who had been admitted to the United Orders by being installed a Knight Templar during the previous year. The Malta degrees are also worked at the November meetings of Great Priory.

Qualifications
Candidates for installation as a Knight Templar must profess the Christian faith, and be both a Master Mason and Royal Arch mason.

Progression
The sequence of offices in a Preceptory is as follows:

Steward
Captain of Guards
Second Standard Bearer
First Standard Bearer
Second Herald
First Herald
Second Constable
First Constable
Preceptor

To qualify for Preceptor, a Knight must have served the office of Constable for a full year. A Preceptor may not continue in office for more than two years in succession.

The Work
Most Preceptories work only one degree, the Installation of a Knight. The ceremony is mainly in the hands of the Preceptor, whose work is roughly equal to that of the Master in the first degree of the Craft, not counting the Charge to the Initiate. The Marshall, the equivalent to a Director of Ceremonies, conducts the candidate and does most of the floor-work. The Captain of the Guard is equivalent to the Inner Guard.

The installation of a Preceptor is mainly in the hands of the outgoing Preceptor and is quite a short ceremony.

With the single exception of the Baldwyn rite practiced in Bristol, there is no ritual variation, the ritual being printed and issued under the authority of the Grand Master's Council.

Cost

The Knight Templar regalia is quite expensive, being approximately ten times that of the Master Mason Craft apron so that many of those about to become Knights attempt to find secondhand items. Several of these, such as the sword, belt, cap, and jewels are durable and do not deteriorate with use.

The cost of the Knight of Malta mantle, tunic, cap and jewel is approximately five times that of the Master Mason Craft apron. It is, however, acceptable for the Templar regalia to be worn in place of the Malta regalia except when taking part in the ceremony. Even then, some Provinces will lend out the necessary regalia for the ceremony.

The fee for installation as Knight is quite low compared to the Craft initiation fee. Details may be obtained from the Treasurer or Registrar of a local Preceptory.

Regalia

The Knight Templar regalia consists of the following:

White tunic with a red cross on the front
White mantle with hood and tassels, and a red cross below the left shoulder
Red cap with a silver cross on the front
Black sash
Two jewels: a Star jewel in silver and a red cross, the latter suspended from a red and white ribbon
A 33 inch straight sword with belt and scabbard
Black gloves

A Preceptor is identified by red hood lining and tassels, and patriarchal cross on the cap and mantle, and the Preceptor's Cross Jewel: a patriarchal cross suspended from the neck by a ribbon. He also carries a baton on which is

Cross Patee

Maltese Cross

Patriarchal Cross

mounted a patriarchal cross. Past Preceptors wear similar regalia but do not carry a baton.

Provincial Officers show their Badge of Office superimposed on the mantle cross, and have a white stripe along the centre of the sash. A Provincial Prior carries a baton with a cross patee and wears a ring on the first finger of the right hand (outside the glove). Within his Province, a Provincial Sub-Prior carries a baton with a patriarchal cross. Similarly, the Jewel of Office which in the Provinces is worn only by the Provincial Prior and Sub-Prior and is suspended from the neck by a ribbon, shows behind the shield a baton with the respective cross.

Great Priory Officers show their Badge of Office superimposed on the mantle cross, have three white stripes along the sash, and a gilt patriarchal cross on the cap.

The Knight of Malta regalia consists of:

Red tunic with a white Maltese cross on the front
Black mantle with a hood and a white Maltese cross below the left shoulder
Black cap with a white Maltese cross on the front
Jewel of white Maltese cross suspended from a black ribbon
Sword, belt and gloves as for Knight Templar

In the Order of Malta, the Prior is identified by the Prior's Cross, which is a white Maltese cross surmounted by a gold crown, suspended from the neck by a ribbon. A similar crown is added to the cross on the cap. A Past Prior is identified by a Maltese cross and crown with a small patriarchal cross and name of the Priory in the centre of the Maltese cross.

Great Priory Officers wear a white Maltese cross surrounded by a black belt containing the name of the Order, and suspended from a black and white ribbon.

Governing Body

The Chancery of the Orders is based at Mark Masons' Hall, 86 St James's Street, London SW1 and has at its head its ME and Supreme Grand Master. It has over 400 Preceptories on its register, of which nearly 130 are overseas. A Provincial organisation similar to that of the Craft is employed, with Provincial Priors appointed with powers similar to those of the Supreme Grand Master. The 20 plus London Preceptories and those not included in a Province are in the charge of the Supreme Grand Master himself. Provincial Priors may appoint to acting Provincial Office and to Past Provincial rank a certain number of Knights from within the Province, the number being dependent on the number of Preceptories in the Province.

Historical Background

The official historical notes on the origin of these degrees explain their appearance in France about 1740 as the result of the Papal Bull of 1738. In France the Bull was more effective than in Protestant England and many French Freemasons, threatened with excommunication, sought a means of combining a Christian background with a Masonic ritual. Thus were born, in their original form, the several degrees which included the Rose-Croix, Knight Templar, Knight of Malta, Royal Arch, and many more.

There is evidence of the degrees being worked in England from about 1770 by Masonic bodies known as Encampments (the equivalent of today's Preceptories). In 1791, Thomas Dunckerley formed a Grand Encampment which became the Grand Conclave of England. The name changes of Encampment to Preceptory, Commander to Preceptor, etc came about as a result of an attempt to amalgamate the Grand Conclaves of England and Wales, Scotland and Ireland. Scotland withdrew at an early stage, and the resulting body, known as Convent General was unpopular and unsuccessful, although its name changes have endured. In 1895, after 23 years, matters returned to normal. The English governing body dropped the 'National' from its title and became simply Great Priory of England and Wales, and autonomous once more. It has increased its Preceptories from 120 in 1900 to nearly 450 today.

The standardisation of the Knight Templar ritual took place during the early 1850s and was based upon a ritual which went back to before 1791. Within a decade the Malta ritual had also been revised and made official.

The need for Royal Arch membership as qualification probably dates from the era, soon after the introduction of the Knight Templar and Knight of Malta ceremonies into England, when they were adopted and worked by Royal Arch Chapters.

The Military Orders

Neither the Knight Templar, nor the Knight of Malta degree has any connection with the Medieval Orders other than being based on their dress and history. The Templars were formed in the early twelfth century following the fall of Jerusalem in 1099, and permanently dissolved by the early fourteenth century. The Order of St John began with a hospice in Jerusalem to tend to the needs of pilgrims visiting the Holy Places. By the early twelfth century, following the example of the Templars, a military group was formed which subsequently expanded to a formidable force. Both military Orders wore monastic slips over their armour; the Templars a white slip with a red cross; the Hospitallers a red slip with a white cross. Both took part in the Crusades until 1291 when the Crusaders were expelled from their positions by the Saracen forces.

The Order of St John settled in Cyprus for a short spell, then moved to Rhodes, where they remained for some 200 years, and finally to Malta for nearly three centuries. During this period the Order remained a military one and had many battles with the Turks, including a famous victory over Suleiman's forces at the siege of Malta in 1565. In 1798 Napoleon annexed Malta and expelled the Order. This signalled the end of the military Order, but the maintenance of a hospital service is still being carried out by the resettled remains of the Order which has its headquarters in Rome, and the revived English Order which founded the St John Ambulance Association in 1877.

Further Reading

1. A small 39-page booklet entitled *The Origin and History of the United Orders* by R. M. Handfield-Jones is published under the authority of the Supreme Grand Master's Council. It is available from masonic suppliers and bookshops. The book describes the development of the United Orders, gives brief histories of the two Medieval Orders, and has, in addition, notes on the rituals.
2. A paper in *AQC* 91 (1978) by John Webb entitled 'The Order of St John and its relationship to Freemasonry' gives a useful overview of the Medieval Order of St John and its revival in England in the nineteenth century. Note, however, that the links with Freemasonry relate to Craft Freemasonry, and not to the Orders of the Temple or Malta.
3. There is also a *Short History of the Order of St John* issued by the present-day (non-Masonic) Order of St John, St John's Gate, London EC1 which has as one of its foundations, the St John Ambulance Association. This book contains an interesting history which includes references to the Templars.
4. A. C. F. Jackson's *Rose Croix: A History of the Ancient and Accepted Rite in England and Wales* contains several pages on the development of Knights Templar Order in England.

ROSE CROIX

The Rose Croix degree is only one of 33 degrees contained in the Ancient and Accepted Rite. It is however the only degree to be worked by private chapters. The degrees of Craft Masonry are considered the equivalent of the first three degrees of the Ancient and Accepted Rite. The 4th to the 17th degrees are conferred by name immediately prior to the Rose Croix or 18th degree ceremony. Degrees higher than the 18th may only be conferred by the Grand Chapter. Here again, the 19th to 29th degrees are conferred by name only, prior to the 30th degree ceremony.

Qualifications
Candidates for the 18th degree must profess the Christian faith, and have been a Master Mason for at least one year.

The qualification for the 30th degree is that of past Sovereign and at least three years service in the 18th degree.

The 31st and 32nd degrees are conferred to selected members only. The 31° requires three years at the 30°, and the 32° requires five years at the 31°. Generally, however, they are conferred on those who have given special service to the Order.

The 33° is usually only conferred on members of the Supreme Council and those who serve as an Inspector General of one of the more than 60 Districts over which the jurisdiction of the Supreme Council extends.

Progression
The sequence of offices in a private chapter is as follows:

Steward
Captain of the Guard
Herald
Almoner
Raphael
Marshal

Second General
First General
Prelate
Sovereign

The office of Prelate is often held by a Past Sovereign. It is partially equivalent to that of Chaplain in the Craft. The Almoner does not participate in the ceremony other than to collect the alms, but the office is nevertheless part of the progression to the chair of Sovereign.

To qualify for Sovereign, a member must have held the office of Prelate, First General or Second General for a year, or be a past Sovereign. No Sovereign may remain in office for more than two years in succession.

The Work

There is only the one degree that is worked, that of perfecting a candidate. The work is almost entirely in the hands of the Sovereign, although Sovereigns will often invite Past Sovereigns to conduct parts of the ceremony. The work to be covered is approximately equal to that of the Master in the first degree of the Craft, not counting the Charge to the Initiate. With the exception of the Prelate, the other offices do not have to cope with more than, say, the work of the Deacons and Inner Guard in a Craft ceremony. There are no ritual differences since, with one exception (the Baldwyn Chapter), all are expected to conform to the printed ritual issued by the Supreme Council.

The Enthronement of the Sovereign in terms of work for the outgoing Sovereign is roughly equal to that of the Installing Master in Craft if the addresses to the Officers are excluded. The incoming Sovereign has very little work during this ceremony since the appointment of Officers is done informally with a few words of thanks in each case. Afterwards, the new Sovereign will conduct that part of the meeting known as the Third Point and, of course, close the Rose Croix Chapter.

Cost

The cost of the collar for the 18th degree is approximately three and a half times that of the Master Mason Craft apron, although a cheaper version without gold thread is also available. Details of the fee for perfection and the annual subscription may be obtained from the Treasurer or Recorder of a local Rose Croix Chapter.

Regalia

The 18th degree regalia consists of a red collar and a jewel. Aprons are no longer used. The collar is richly embroidered with gold thread. A Sovereign of a Chapter also wears a red ribbon round the neck from which a red enamel Greek cross is suspended.

The other degrees are identified as follows:

30° Black sash from left shoulder to right hip
31° White collar
32° Black collar
33° White sash from left shoulder to right hip

These are all embroidered with the emblems of the respective degrees. The 33° regalia includes a black cap.

Governing Body

The Supreme Council 33° for England and Wales and its Districts and Chapters overseas is based at 10 Duke Street, St James', London SW1. The Supreme Council consists of nine members. When a vacancy occurs, a new member, who must be a Grand Officer or Past Grand Officer of the United Grand Lodge, is elected by the remaining eight members. The ties with the United Grand Lodge are strong, and any member who is expelled by the United Grand Lodge is automatically expelled by the Supreme Council. The number of private chapters at the time of writing are close to 900, many of them overseas.

Chapters are organised into Districts where possible, and there are at present nearly 70 such Districts, 38 of them in

England and Wales. The largest of the latter is West Lancashire with 32 Chapters. There are five Districts within the London Group of Chapters, covering some 70 Chapters. A District is not, however, the equivalent to a Province or District in the Craft in the sense of having a regional organisation. It exists mainly to receive, in the first instance, applications, returns, complaints, etc; to provide supervision over the Chapters contained within its boundaries; and, in overseas Districts, to form Grand Chapters of the 30th degree. Each District is supervised by an Inspector General who may be assisted by a District Recorder.

Historical background

The early development of the Ancient and Accepted Rite took place in France following the spread of Freemasonry to France during the first decades of the eighteenth century.

Some of the degrees of the Ancient and Accepted Rite were in existence from as early as 1740 but the collection of the degrees into a complete Rite took place during the second half of the eighteenth century. By 1760, a Rite of Perfection had evolved which consisted of 25 degrees. By 1801, when the first Supreme Council for the Ancient and Accepted Rite was formed at Charleston, South Carolina, the number of degrees had increased to 33.

The transition from France to America occurred during the 1760s through the activities of a French mason, Stephen Morin, whose business caused him to travel between Bordeaux and the West Indies. Morin, empowered from France to promote Freemasonry in the New World, appointed several Inspectors both in the West Indies and America. The Rite was introduced into South Carolina in 1783.

The French Revolution had removed any control of the Rite from France, and in 1801 the Americans in Carolina formed their own governing body, an American Supreme Council.

In 1813 this Supreme Council set up a Supreme Council for

the Northern Jurisdiction of the United States, and itself took the title of Supreme Council for the Southern Jurisdiction. The Supreme Council for England and Wales was formed in 1845 when Dr Robert Crucefix, founder of the RMBI, applied for a patent from the Northern Jurisdiction Supreme Council.

Further Reading

A recent publication which contains a very detailed examination of the development of the Ancient and Accepted Rite, together with much general material in connection with its administration, is *Rose Croix* by Brig A. C. F. Jackson, a member of the Quatuor Coronati Lodge.

MARK AND ROYAL ARK MARINER

The Mark degree consists of two parts, Mark Man and Mark Master, both taking place on the same occasion. Outwardly it is very close to the Craft, for it shares with the Craft its terminology eg 'Lodge', titles of Officers, etc and the setting of the ceremony which is based on an event during the building of King Solomon''s temple.

The degree is conferred, however, by an Order which is completely independent from the Craft and which, moreover, governs the degree of Royal Ark Mariner, as well as providing the administration for several other Orders.

Qualifications

A candidate for admission to the Order must be a Master Mason. Also, to qualify for the chair of Worshipful Master it is necessary to have been installed a Master of a Craft Lodge, although this may be overcome by dispensation.

Progression

The sequence of Offices leading to that of Worshipful Master is as follows:

Steward
Inner Guard
Junior Deacon
Senior Deacon
Junior Overseer
Senior Overseer
Master Overseer
Junior Warden
Senior Warden
Worshipful Master

Qualification, other than that already given, for installation as Worshipful Master is a full year's service as Warden.

The Work

The single degree is the ceremony of Advancement. The work is roughly equal to that of the first degree in Craft Masonry, particularly in the case of the Master. The work of conducting the candidate is given to the Senior Deacon who has, however, a more substantial role than the equivalent position in a Craft degree. There are three extra offices, those of the Overseers, who each have as much work as, say, a Warden in a Craft Ceremony.

A single official ritual is issued by The Grand Lodge of Mark Master Masons and most Lodges adhere to this, although some retain their own workings.

Cost

The cost of the Mark regalia is approximately equal to that of a Master Mason apron. The fee for advancement is generally quite low.

The current fee together with the cost of an annual

subscription may be obtained from the Treasurer or Secretary of a local Mark Master Mason's Lodge.

Regalia

Description: The regalia is similar to that of the Craft but includes a breast jewel. The apron is edged with light blue and crimson, and the rosettes share these colours. The breast jewel is in the form of a keystone suspended by a light blue and crimson ribbon with a silver bar each end.

Rank: Some, but not all the differences in regalia are given below to enable one to identify various ranks.

The aprons of Masters and Past Masters have levels in place of rosettes as in the Craft.

Officers of the Lodge show the emblem of their office on a keystone jewel suspended from collars of light blue and crimson. The collars of Past Masters have a silver braid running down the centre. Officers and past Officers may also have the emblems of their office in the centre of the apron.

Provincial Grand Officers and Holders of London Mark Grand Rank wear collars and aprons with dark blue in place of light blue, and with edging of gold braid and gold fringe (full dress) or gold cord (undress).

Grand Officers wear collars with dark blue in the centre, with either a vertical strip of gold braid and no edging (undress) or embroidered with rose leaves and hyssop, and with gold edging (full dress). Their aprons also show a wreath of rose leaves and hyssop.

Provincial Grand Masters and their Deputies and Assistants wear chains. The jewel of the above is enclosed in a circle.

The jewel of the Grand Master, Pro Grand Master, Deputy Grand Master and Assistant Grand Master contains the Compasses extended to 45° , unenclosed by a circle.

Governing Body

The Grand Lodge of Mark Master Masons is based at Mark Masons' Hall, 86 St James's Street, London SW1. An organisation similar to that of the United Grand Lodge is employed in having Provincial and District Grand Masters, as well as a system of rank of present and past Officers. The Constitutions and Regulations specify the number of appointments to such Office in accordance with the number of Lodges in each Province or District. There is also a London Mark Grand Rank.

A General Board controls the buildings, finances, employees and administration of Grand Lodge, and reports to Grand Lodge at its regular meetings.

There are over 1,300 Mark Lodges on its Roll, plus nearly 700 Royal Ark Mariner Lodges. Other Orders which are administered from within the Grand Lodge of Mark Master Masons include Allied Masonic Degrees, Royal and Select Masters and Red Cross of Constantine.

Historical Background

The traditions of Mark Masonry is based on the system of allocating a mark to each individual operative mason and his subsequent use of it on stone on which he has worked. This system dates back to medieval days, although builders' marks are also to be found on stonework of ancient buildings in Egypt, Greece, etc.

Speculative Mark Masonry itself cannot, however, be traced further back than the late eighteenth century. It is possible that the degree originated earlier in the century in Scotland where biblical references to the rejection of a stone may have been joined with the tradition of mason's marks to form a symbolical ceremony in the mould of speculative Masonry, but the earliest clear reference to the working of a Mark degree occurs in the minute book of the Chapter of Friendship, Portsmouth for September 1769.

Initially, the Mark degree was worked by Craft Lodges and Royal Arch Chapters. At the formation of the United Grand Lodge in 1813, the Royal Arch was given recognition while other degrees, including that of Mark, were not. The Mark was thus effectively debarred from being worked in

Craft Lodges or Royal Arch Chapters. Mark Lodges were formed in their own right, but they were irregular and there was little incentive for Craft or RA Masons to join them.

In 1851, a Mark Lodge (Bon Accord) was started in London which was to result in the formation of a Mark Grand Lodge. It received its charter from a Scottish RA Chapter in Aberdeen (Bon Accord RA Chapter) and was so successful that five years later it had a membership of 120. Indeed, its very success resulted in a dispute between the Grand Chapter of Scotland and the Aberdeen Bon Accord RA Chapter which ended in the suspension and closing of the latter. In 1856 the United Grand Lodge first resolved, and then at the next meeting reversed the decision, that the degree of Mark Mason or Mark Master could form a part of Craft Masonry. Within weeks of the reversal, members of the London Bon Accord met and reached a decision to begin a Grand Mark Lodge.

The early existence of this self-proclaimed Grand Mark Lodge was uncertain, but ten years after its inception it had 86 Mark Lodges on its roll. By its twenty-fifth year the number of its Lodges had grown to 282. In 1886, the Prince of Wales, who had been Grand Master of the Craft since 1874, was installed as Mark Grand Master and remained in both positions until his coronation as Edward VII in 1901. Today, the Mark degree ranks with that of the Royal Arch as the two most popular non-Craft degrees.

Royal Ark Mariner

Every RAM Lodge is attached to a Mark Lodge, and often its meetings will follow that of a Mark Lodge on the same day. The qualification for admission to RAM is naturally that of Mark Master Mason.

The regalia consists of an apron and breast jewel. The ceremoney of Elevation in the RAM degree is quite short and is based on the legend of Noah's Ark. References to Noah occur in the earliest manuscript Charges (see Old Charges), starting with the *Regius MS* of c1390. The degree itself, however, does not appear to have been in existence much before the late eighteenth century.

The Royal Ark Mariner degree was taken under the protection of the Mark Grand Lodge in 1871, and is governed by the Grand Master with advice from a Royal Ark Council, which is the equivalent of the General Board of the Mark Grand Lodge. Since 1968, Grand and London/ Provincial/District Grand Rank has been awarded in recognition of services to the RAM degree.

Further Reading

1. *History of the Grand Lodge of Mark Master Masons* by R. M. Handfield-Jones. This is the official history published under the authority of the General Board of the Mark Grand Lodge. The content is mainly concerned with the foundation and events surrounding the development of the Grand Lodge of Mark Master Masons up to 1968 when the book was completed.
2. *The Royal Ark Mariner Degree: Its Origin and History* by R. M. Handfield-Jones. This booklet of some 30 plus pages covers the story of the Flood, the transmission of the Noah story in drama, various opinions on the origin of the degree, details of references to the degree prior to 1850, the circumstances leading up to the protection of the RAM degree by the Mark Grand Lodge, and progress since then.

OTHER MASONIC ORDERS

There are several other Masonic Orders which, while not as well-known as those described earlier, draw many Craft masons into their respective circles. The qualifications for admission to some of these Orders are given below:

Order	*Qualification*
Red Cross of Constantine	: Royal Arch Mason
Knights Templar Priests	: Past Master of the Craft, Royal Arch Mason, and Knight Templar
Royal Order of Scotland	: Minimum: Master Mason of five years standing
Order of the Secret Monitor	: Master Mason
Royal and Select Masters (Cryptic Degrees)	: Mark Master Mason, and Royal Arch Mason
Order of the Allied Masonic Degrees	: Mark Master Mason, and Royal Arch Mason

Those wishing to know more of these Orders and their Degrees are advised to consult *Beyond the Craft* by Keith Jackson.

GREAT QUEEN STREET

GREAT QUEEN STREET

The headquarters of English Freemasonry since 1776, this ancient thoroughfare runs between Drury Lane in the west and Kingsway in the east, with Lincoln's Inn Fields a short walk further east. The name Great Queen Street came into use during the second half of the seventeenth century, but records show the names of occupants of houses in the street from as early as 1611.

It became the home of English Freemasonry with the erection of the first Freemasons' Hall in 1776. The Duke of Beaufort had become Grand Master in 1767 and shortly afterwards proposed the raising of a fund which would enable the erection of a hall for the purposes of providing a central place for Lodges to hold their meetings. In 1774, Grand Lodge purchased two large dwelling-houses together with a garden at No 61 Great Queen Street for the sum of £3,180. Here, at No 61, the first Freemasons' Hall was built by the architect Sandby. It was opened on the 23 May 1776 by Lord Petre who had succeeded the Duke of Beaufort in 1772. A continuous history of expansion and rebuilding followed, until today the Masonic occupation of the south side of Great Queen Street runs from No 47 to No 65. The third and most recent Freemasons' Hall was completed in 1933, occupying all but Nos 61 to 65, which is today the address of the Connaught Rooms, one of the Masonic dining centres of London.

Masonic concerns are also to be found on the north side of Great Queen Street. At No 19/21 are Toye, Kenning & Spencer Ltd, regalia manufacturers, and the offices of the three Masonic Charities are on the north side:

- The Royal Masonic Benevolent Institution (RMBI) at No 20
- The Royal Masonic Institution for Boys at No 26
- The Royal Masonic Institution for Girls at No 31

No 27 was for many years the headquarters of the Quatuor Coronati Lodge from where the well-known Correspondence Circle was administered. Today this eminent lodge of research operates from within Freemasons' Hall.

No 33 contains the offices of the London Grand Rank Association. The publishers of the periodical *Masonic Record*, now no longer published, used to occupy No 38.

At Freemasons' Hall are held the meetings of several London Lodges, Provincial Grand Lodges and, of course, Grand Lodge itself. Other major attractions within Freemasons' Hall are the Library and Museum.

Great Queen Street is reached by Underground to Holborn Station, or by car with underground parking in Parker Street or Wild Street. It is also possible to park on the perimeter of Lincoln's Inn Fields or across Drury Lane in Covent Garden or, occasionally, at one of the parking meters in Great Queen Street itself. Further parking is available at Bloomsbury Square.

FREEMASONS' HALL

The history of Freemasons' Hall in Great Queen Street begins in 1774 with the acquisition by Grand Lodge of the property at No 61 Great Queen Street. The architect Thomas Sandby designed a Hall which was erected at a cost of some £15,000. This being more expensive than anticipated, the 'Hall Debt' was partially paid off by a scheme which required a subscription of £25 or more from brethren or lodges in exchange for which a Medal or Jewel would be presented to such subscribers.

In 1815, two more houses to the east of No 61 were acquired by Grand Lodge. The buildings were internally connected and expanded by additional building behind the original premises. In 1863, Grand Lodge who had meanwhile purchased properties to the west and east of the Hall, decided to erect a new, larger structure. The foundation stone of the second Freemasons' Hall was laid on the 27 April 1864.

Vacant possession was obtained in 1899 of two houses to the west of the new Hall, which had been purchased in 1858. These were demolished and the masonic premises extended westwards, giving a permanent home to the Library and Museum. Also in 1899, Grand Lodge purchased two more properties, giving it an ownership of properties running from No 55 to 65. Plans to utilise the new acquisitions were delayed first by attempts to preserve the fronts of the buildings, and then by the First World War. Work ceased in 1917.

In 1919, the idea was broached by the Grand Master, the Duke of Connaught, of erecting a Peace Memorial to the many brethren who had fallen in the War, in the form of a new home for Freemasonry. As a result, the planned structure became known as the Masonic Peace Memorial. A fund, known as the Masonic Million Memorial Fund was started. The methods by which the target of a million pounds was achieved, and which led to the creation of the Hall Stone Jewel are described on pages 73–4.

At first there was much argument as to the site of the proposed Peace Memorial, the third Freemasons' Hall. One school was in favour of remaining at Great Queen Street with its traditional associations, another in favour of a more impressive site on the Thames embankment, the Adelphi site. Late in 1920, however, Grand Lodge authorised the purchase of more properties to the west of the existing Hall. Grand Lodge now owned all properties to the west of No 61 bounded by Great Queen Street, Wild Street, and Wild Court which runs off Wild Street to the back of the present structure. The extra space this provided, together with the historical associations, decided matters in favour of Great Queen Street, and in 1927 the foundation stone ceremony took place.

A book entitled *Freemasons' Hall*, available from the

Grand Lodge Library or the Enquiries Office, contains useful information about the building and its contents, and has many coloured photographs.

The Library and Museum are open to any visitor on weekdays between the hours of 10 am to 5 pm, Saturdays 10 am to 1 pm, except on public holidays and the Saturday preceding these. The Grand Temple may be visited from 11 am to 4 pm on the hour at hourly intervals, Mondays to Fridays, parties being conducted from the museum. Only one pre-arranged party visit takes place on Saturdays, at 10.30 am. Intending visitors on the Saturday visit should check with the Grand Secretary's office in advance. Ladies and non-masons may visit the Hall if they are accompanied by members of the Craft.

The building occupies an area of over two acres, the first floor containing the major rooms, including the magnificent Grand Temple, the Library and the Museum. The approach to the Grand Temple is through the Temple Entrance at the corner of Great Queen Street and Wild Street. Winding staircases lead to the three vestibules which serve as anterooms to the Grand Temple. The walls of the ground floor entrance hall and above it contain the lists of the Hall Stone Lodges.

The second and third floors contain 19 Lodge rooms and there are two, smaller, Lodge rooms on a mezzanine. These, together with the Library, Museum and Enquiries Office, are reached through the entrance in Great Queen Street.

The large Enquiries Office is situated on the ground floor. The staff are accustomed to deal with visitors, either local or from abroad, even to the extent of calling on the help of an interpreter to assist with a non-English-speaking visitor. The Enquiries Office provides much of the standard Masonic reference material such as the *Year Book*, *Book of Constitutions*, Circulars, Slides, and Extracts from the Proceedings of Grand Lodge.

GRAND LODGE LIBRARY AND MUSEUM

The Grand Lodge library and museum were formed in 1837 when £100 was voted for the purpose of starting the collection. Little was done until 1880 when R. F. Gould, who wrote the unique *History of Freemasonry*, influenced his colleagues on the Board of General Purposes to improve matters. An annual grant of £25 was approved in 1882 and the Library Committee was added as a permanent sub-committee to the Board of General Purposes. A further major step forward was taken with the appointment in 1887 of a Grand Lodge Librarian and Curator. The first occupant of this office, at first designated sub-librarian, was Henry Sadler, who was vigorous in building up the collection of books, documents and exhibits, laying the foundation for the present library of some 35,000 volumes and the extensive collection of documents, art, jewels, regalia, and objects of masonic significance.

The library is a reference library only, and is arranged in a series of bays, each bay containing a table and chair. Scrap paper is thoughtfully provided for those who want to make notes.

The books are held in glass-fronted cabinets which are kept locked unless being used. A library attendant is on hand to show visitors to the cabinet containing the books they wish to consult and to unlock the sliding glass fronts.

The collection of rituals and English Exposures is kept in a separate room in order to maintain a control over it, while valuable and antiquarian books are kept in a strongroom but may be requested. Card index systems, by author and by subject, are maintained and may be used by visitors to the Library.

The classification system is unique to the Masonic library and was developed in the early 1960s by A. R. Hewitt, the then Grand Lodge Librarian and Curator. He devised a system to suit the particular needs of Freemasonry, since the standard Dewey Library Classification system would have been unworkable.

The system is based on divisions by country or territory, eg BE for England or BS for Scotland, and class or subject eg 910 for Periodicals. Thus BE910 refers to periodicals in England, while BS910 refers to periodicals in Scotland. The class code is completed by a suffix which indicates the author or issuing body, eg CAR for Cartwright. In certain cases the classification codes are supplemented by additional information eg BE60 (LIN) DIX is the code for a *History of Freemasonry in Lincolnshire* by W. Dixon.

The main class headings are:

10–29	:	General Works on Freemasonry
30–89	:	History and Philosophy of Freemasonry
90–179	:	Government and Organisation of the Craft
180–229	:	Symbolism, Ritual and Ceremonial
230–259	:	Regalia, Jewels and Documents
300–450	:	Royal Arch
460–700	:	Additional Degrees
705–709	:	Masonic Clubs and Associations
710–720	:	Benevolence
725–727	:	Education
730–750	:	Masonic Music, Poetry, Plays, Rhetoric
760–780	:	The Fine Arts in Masonry
790–800	:	Anti-Masonry and Vindication
805–819	:	Irregular, Spurious and Clandestine Masonry
820–845	:	Women in Freemasonry
850–885	:	Negro Freemasonry
910	:	Periodicals

Classification codes of 1000 and higher cover allied and general literature, eg 1250 to 1420 for Philosophy and Religion, 1450 to 1700 for Social Sciences, etc.

Within a Class, the books are arranged according to the surnames of the authors, unless they are first grouped by Province.

The museum collection is classified into the following main categories:

Silverware and gold plate
Other metalware
Porcelain and pottery
Glassware
Watches and clocks
Snuff-boxes, pipes and smokers' requisites
Jewels
Furniture
Bric-a-brac
Regalia

Of particular interest are the many gifts received by the United Grand Lodge, both from individuals and other Grand Lodges. One such is a gift from the Queen, a casket of Indian silver which had been presented to the Prince of Wales, later Edward VII, by the Masons of Bengal. The silver is decorated with Craft and Royal Arch emblems in gold. Also to be seen are the two Chi'en Lung period porcelain punch-bowls presented by King George V after a visit in 1934 by the King and Queen to the newly opened Freemasons' Hall.

There are also Print and Document collections. The period covered by organised Masonry, 1717 onwards, ensures that apart from their Masonic interest, many items are also of special interest to students of antique porcelain, glassware, clock movements, and the work of silversmiths and goldsmiths.

QUATUOR CORONATI LODGE

This well-known lodge of research meets five times a year at Freemasons' Hall. It has a very small membership, limited to 40, but usually below thirty since membership is by invitation only to those who have made important contributions in the field of masonic research or distinguished themselves in the arts and sciences. The meetings are, however, also attended by members of the QC Correspondence Circle (see under the section on Education).

Other than the annual installation of a new Master and the Opening and Closing of the Lodge, no ceremonies are conducted. The meetings are instead given over to the delivery of papers on masonic subjects. Indeed, the Installation is itself followed by the presentation of an inaugural address by the new Master. The papers often arouse lively comments from other members present, which provide useful side-lights on the subject.

The meetings are held on the third Thursday in February, second Thursday in May, September and November (Installation), and fourth Thursday in June, always at 5 pm.

LONDON GRAND RANK ASSOCIATION

The London Grand Rank Association, which is based at 33 Great Queen Street, has been in existence since 1909. It came into being following the first appointments to London Rank in 1908. These had been introduced to give recognition to members of London Lodges for merit and service, equivalent to Provincial and District Grand Rank.

Initially, the Association was seen as a means whereby holders of London Rank could meet to exchange information and discuss common interests. Shortly afterwards an arrangement was introduced whereby votes in favour of London applicants for benefits or relief from the Charities, could be pooled as they were in the Provinces. In 1939 the word 'Grand' was introduced to put the title on par with those in the Provinces.

The London Grand Rank Association has a membership in excess of 9,500 representing nearly 1,700 London Lodges.

Quarterly (non- ceremonial) meetings are held at which the main item on the agenda consists of a Talk or the presentation of a Paper. These are reprinted in the Quarterly Bulletin which is issued to all members, but may also be obtained for a small fee by members of Provincial Lodges.

The Association maintains a team of lecturers to assist Lodges in supplying information to their members, gives guidance on procedure, operates a blanket Covenant Scheme for Masonic Charities, and provides several other services to its members. A London Grand Rank Fund exists to extend relief to Master Masons of London Lodges, or their widows.

MEETINGS

THE TYLER

The duties of a Tyler extend beyond those of guarding the Lodge externally and preparing the candidates. He is in charge of the articles belonging to the Lodge, and responsible for setting out the lodge and ensuring that everything that will be needed is in place. Once the brethren arrive, he is there to see to them and their visitors and to render any service such as supplying an apron found wanting. He should, ideally, ensure that everyone signs the attendance book.

During the meeting, the Tyler signals by his knocks whether it is a late-comer or the candidate that seeks admission. He also plays host to the candidate and tries to make him feel at home. Tylers have often stated that they particularly enjoy looking after a prospective Initiate, performing the very necessary role of reassuring someone who faces an unknown situation in a strange environment. Many Tylers take particular pride in ensuring that candidates for higher degrees are able to communicate correctly their signs, tokens and words.

After the meeting the Tyler is responsible for removing and securing the articles used for the meeting. Lastly, he is required at the close of the festive board for the final toast, the Tyler's toast:

> To all poor and distressed Masons, wherever dispersed over the face of earth, and water, wishing them a speedy relief from all their sufferings, and a safe return to their native country, if they desire it.

There are variations on these words dating from as early as 1756, although they were not then associated with a Tyler.

The Tyler's toast is often followed by a variation on:

Dear brethren of the Mystic Tie,
    the night is waning fast
Our duty's done – our feast is o'er
    this song must be our last:
'Good Night' 'Good Night' – Once more, once
    more repeat the farewell strain –
'Happy to meet, Sorry to part,
    Happy to meet again!'

It is the final stanza of a poem entitled *The Final Toast* written by D. L. Richardson in India in the middle of the previous century. The practice of its following the time-hallowed final toast is, however, illogical and many would prefer it to be abandoned or, at the very least, have it precede the Tyler's toast.

When calling on the Tyler, either during the meeting or at table, the Master gives the Tyler's knocks : two knocks which are nowhere else used.

BIBLE OPENINGS

The expression refers to the pages at which the VSL is opened after the WM has declared the Lodge open. While there is no requirement upon a Lodge to open the VSL at any particular page, there are several customary openings such as *Psalm* 133 for the first degree:

> Behold, how good and how pleasant it is for brethren to dwell together in unity!

Other bible openings include the First Book of *Kings*, Chapter 6, Verse 8 which refers to the 'winding stairs into the middle chamber', and *Judges*, Chapter 12, which tells the brief story of Jephthah and how he dealt with the Ephraimites.

Bristol working is unusual in that it specifies the pages to be opened, the Master quoting them during the Openings of the degrees. They are *Ruth*, Chapter 2, Verse 19 for the first degree; *Judges*, Chapter 12, Verses 6 and 7 for the second; and *Genesis*, Chapter 4, Verse 22 for the third.

In the degrees of other Orders the bible may be opened at particular reference points, such as the Knights Templar degree where the bibles are opened at the Gospel of St John.

REGALIA

An official and very detailed description of regalia to be worn by members of the Craft in English Constitution lodges is given in the *Book of Constitutions.* Briefly, however, the following outline will serve to identify the differences to be observed in the regalia of those attending private Lodges:

Private Lodges

APRONS	Entered Apprentice	White, unadorned
	Fellow Craft	White, adorned with two rosettes
	Master Mason	White, with light blue edging, three rosettes, and silver tassels on light blue strings.
	Master and Past Master	As Master Mason but in place of the rosettes, three silver levels.
COLLARS	Officers of the Lodge	Light blue
	Past Masters	Light blue with silver braid in the centre. Only Past Masters may wear their collars when visiting other Lodges. The Master and his Wardens may wear their collars

when attending Grand Lodge or Provincial Grand Lodge.

JEWELS Officers Affixed to collars, these designate the office of the wearer:

Master	:	Square
Senior Warden	:	Level
Junior Warden	:	Plumb rule
Chaplain	:	Open Book
Treasurer	:	Key
Secretary	:	Two feather pens tied by a ribbon
Director of Ceremonies	:	Two rods tied by a ribbon
Senior Deacon	:	Dove and olive branch
Junior Deacon	:	Dove and olive branch
Charity Steward	:	Trowel
Almoner	:	Purse
Asst. D.C.	:	Two rods with the word 'Assistant'
Organist	:	Lyre
Asst. Secretary	:	Two feather pens with the word 'Assistant'
Inner Guard	:	Two swords
Steward	:	Cornucopia and Compasses

Past Masters wear the Square with the 47th proposition of the First Book of Euclid.

Provincial Grand Officers
(The following does not apply to Provincial Grand Stewards)

APRONS	Officers, present and past	As Masters, but with 2-inch dark (garter) blue edging and strings, and gold decoration in place of silver. The emblem of their office is shown in the centre of the apron within a double circle, which also contains the name of the Province.
COLLARS	Officers, present and past	Dark blue (garter-blue) edges with either gold lace (thick edging) or gold cord (thin edging). The Provincial Grand Master and his Deputy or Assistant(s) wear a chain in place of a collar.
JEWELS	Officers, present	The emblem of his office enclosed within a double *circle* with the name of the Province engraved within the double circle.
	Officers, past	The emblem of his office on a blue enamelled *oval* together with the name of the Province.

The above does not apply in full to Provincial Grand Stewards, present and past, who wear a crimson (and narrower) collar and have a crimson edging to their aprons. Past Provincial Grand Stewards have a silver cord running down the centre of the collar, and a red enamelled background to their jewel.

London and Overseas Grand Rank

This regalia is as that for Provincial Grand Officers but without any emblem of office. London Grand Rank (and Overseas Grand Rank) has the square with the 47th proposition of the First Book of Euclid to identify it, while Senior London Grand Rank has a square, level and plumb rule as jewel and on the apron.

Grand Officers

APRONS As Provincial Officers but with three and one half inch edging and with the emblem of office shown within a wreath formed of a sprig of acacia and ear of corn. Provincial Grand Masters have the name of their Province above the emblem of office.

COLLARS Garter-blue, plain with no edging, or embroidered with gold edging and a sprig of acacia and an ear of corn running down the collar. In Grand Lodge the present Grand Officers wear chains in place of collars.

JEWELS As Provincial Officers except that the double circle or oval contains the sprig of acacia and ear of corn in place of the name of the Province.

Grand Stewards are identified by four inch crimson edging to their aprons, and a crimson collar, the latter with silver cord edging if they are Past Grand Stewards.

Full Dress and Undress

The aprons and collars of Provincial Grand Officers, Holders of London Grand Rank, and Grand Officers may take two forms: full dress to be worn at meetings of Grand and Provincial Grand Lodge, and undress to be used at meetings of private Lodges. Individual Lodge or Provincial custom may, however, dictate that only one form is used. Undress is always the plainer of the two, eg a Grand rank collar without gold edging or the sprigs of corn and acacia. Full dress aprons are ornamented with gold lace and gold fringe around the edging and the triangular flap.

HALL STONE LODGES & THE HALL STONE JEWEL

The story of the Hall Stone Jewel begins in 1919 at a meeting of Grand Lodge held specially to celebrate the end of the First World War. The Grand Master, the Duke of Connaught, suggested the creation of a 'perpetual memorial of the Craft's gratitude to Almighty God' and 'to render fitting honour to the many brethren who fell during the war'. He suggested that the most fitting memorial would be the erection of a central home for Freemasonry.

A target figure of one million pounds, a staggering figure in those days, was set to cover the cost of building the proposed memorial. An appeal went out to all Lodges and brethren to subscribe to the scheme by contributing to the fund, which soon became known as the Masonic Million Memorial Fund. The appeal included a facsimile of a personal letter from the Grand Master and an explanation of the intended method of giving recognition for contributions. The method that was eventually decided upon provided for the issue of a medal, the Hall Stone medal: 'Every Lodge whose total list, including its own donation, amounts to an average of Ten Guineas per member, shall be recorded in the Building as a HALL STONE LODGE, and its Master shall be entitled to wear a special Medal as a collarette, whilst acting as WM of the Lodge.'

There were other means of obtaining the medal such as individual subscriptions, but the most enduring legacy has been left by that described above.

The names of the Hall Stone Lodges are recorded on the walls of the entrance hall of the Grand Temple in the

Masonic Peace Memorial, the present Freemasons' Hall.

The design of the medal was decided following an open competition which was won by Bro Cyril Spackman. The jewel is in the form of a cross with squared ends and the dates 1914–1918 in the squares on the horizontal arms. Between these is the winged figure of Peace supporting a temple. The medal is suspended by the Square and Compasses.

In 1925, a Festival was held at Olympia to revive the flagging interest in the Memorial Fund. A contribution of £15.75, which could include any previous contribution, was required for admission to the Festival dinner. Over 7,000 brethren attended. The Grand Master was there to take wine with those who came, and the Grand Secretary read the lists of contributions to the Masonic Million Memorial Fund. The figure had by then risen to £826,014.

The foundation stone for the new Hall was laid in 1927, and the building opened in 1933, but the process of finishing and furnishing rooms continued for some years. The fund was closed in 1939 having exceeded its target by a third of a million pounds.

Today, there are still nearly 1,300 Lodges on the Register of the United Grand Lodge, who have received a Hall Stone Lodge Jewel, the highest number being that of the Zeus Lodge No 5418.

ANNO LUCIS

Anno Lucis is converted to Anno Domini by subtracting 4,000. This form of dating assumes that the world had been created 4,000 years when Christ was born. Thus, the explanation of the Third Degree Tracing Board states that Hiram Abif was slain 3,000 years after the creation of the world. Until scientific investigation showed that the age of the world should be measured not in thousands, but in thousands of millions of years, estimates of the date of the Creation were based on biblical material.

In the seventeenth century a chronology based on information contained in the Old Testament, the *Annales Veteris*, was produced by James Ussher, who became Archbishop of Armagh. Ussher's chronology put the birth of Christ 4,004 years after the Creation. His form of dating became popular through its use in the margins of the 1701 edition of the Bible and in many subsequent editions. The variant of 4,000 is also to be found, starting with an edition of the Bible which was printed in 1679. The Hebrew calendar employs a similar form of dating, but has the Creation at 3,760 BC, not 4,000 or 4,004.

When James Anderson produced the first *Constitutions* in 1723, he employed this form of dating, giving both 1723 and 5723 as the date, but called the latter 'In the Year of Masonry'. It has since become a tradition in Craft Masonry, and appears on every Grand Lodge Certificate. The Scottish Constitution follows a similar tradition but uses Ussher's system of adding 4,004 to the Anno Domini date.

Anno Lucis means 'In the year of Light'. The term will not be found outside Masonry, since Anno Mundi, ie in the year of the world, is commonly used to describe the same system. The use of the former may have come about in the following way:

The Latin for Anderson's 'In the Year of Masonry', ie Anno Latomiae, was abbreviated to AL and this abbreviation was commonly used on masonic documents of the late eighteenth century. Later AL came to be regarded as Anno Lucis, possibly as a result of the influence of Masonic customs in France where the French phrase for 'In the year of Light' was used on the majority of Masonic documents, particularly those of the 'higher' degrees.

Today, Anno Lucis is internationally used as a form of dating by Freemasons.

COUNTRY MEMBERS

The expression refers to brethren who are permitted a

reduced subscription which excludes a dining fee. It probably derives from members who live some distance from their Lodge, ie in the country, and who could not attend meetings regularly. When they did attend, they would pay a dining fee equal to that paid for a visitor.

In practice, the term covers any brother who wishes to retain membership of his Lodge, but does not expect to attend many of its meetings. The expression 'non-dining members' as an alternative is often encountered.

RELIGIOUS DENOMINATIONS

Craft Freemasonry is open to men of all religious denominations. In the eyes of the Craft, persuasions of Protestant, Jewish, or Catholic nature, as do many others, have in common a belief in a Supreme Being. A statement entitled *Aims and Relationships of the Craft* and issued by the Grand Lodges of England, Ireland and Scotland in 1938 contains an outline of the fundamental principles of the Order, the first of which was stated as follows:

> The first condition of admission into, and membership of, the Order is a belief in the Supreme Being. This is essential and admits of no compromise.

The *Book of Constitutions* goes further. In the first section of 'The Charges of a Free-Mason' it states:

> Let a man's religion or mode of worship be what it may, he is not excluded from the order, provided he believe in the glorious architect of heaven and earth, and practise the sacred duties of morality.

The Old Charges contain Trinitarian Christian references, but by 1723, in Anderson's *Constitutions*, the following occurs:

> 'tis now thought more expedient only to oblige them [Masons] to

> that Religion in which all Men agree, leaving their particular Opinions to themselves; that is, to be *good Men and true*, or Men of Honour and Honesty, by whatever Denominations or Persuasions they may be distinguis'd; . . .

At that time the major faiths of England were Christian. Today, the Christian references which originally appeared in the ritual are no longer to be found. They were probably excised from the ritual shortly after the Union in 1813 of the Modern and Antient Grand Lodges, when the Lodge of Reconciliation set to work settling the differences between the two workings. The one obvious reference which escaped excision is to 'that bright morning star' which refers to Christ and is a quotation from *Revelation*, Chapter 22, Verse 16:

> I Jesus have sent mine angel to testify unto you these things in the churches. I am the root and the offspring of David, and the bright and morning star.

Roman Catholics have had their own problems in being permitted entry to the Order. It has not been until recent years that the Papal Bulls of earlier centuries have been relaxed. These prohibited Catholics from participating in meetings of freemasons since Freemasonry was, with others, termed a secret society. Today, a Catholic still has to obtain the consent of his bishop to become a Craft freemason, but at least the opportunity exists.

A candidate who is of a faith which does not have the Bible as its sacred Book, may choose to take his obligations on his own Volume of the Sacred Law such as, for example, the Koran for a Moslem, or the Bhagavad Gita for a Hindu.

BLACK BALL

This phrase refers to a method of balloting whereby each member of the Lodge receives a black and a white ball (or bean) the white being used to cast a vote in favour, the black against the proposal. In balloting for the acceptance of a candidate for initiation or a joining member, the black is synonymous with exclusion. This method is found, for example, in the Lodges of South Wales. Another commonly found method is the use of a 'Yea' and 'Nay' drawer whereby each member in the Lodge receives a single ball which is deposited in the appropriate drawer by the insertion of the hand inside a central opening which permits access to either drawer. After the vote, the Master inspects the 'Nay' drawer to see whether any votes had been cast against the candidate.

Any balls in the 'Nay' drawer are still referred to as 'black balls'. Rule 165 in the *Book of Constitutions* declares that, unless the By-laws of the Lodge state otherwise, three black balls constitute a rejection on ballot.

WORKINGS

A wide variety or different workings exists. The ritual traditions of some Lodges date back to before the existence of the United Grand Lodge, while those of others originated during the nineteenth century in a period when, with much reliance on memory and no injunction to maintain the ceremonies in precise detail, the ritual was transmitted as best possible. A working may have been carried in its original form by Lodge founder members from one part of the country to another, to be subsequently changed by local influences. For example, the Lodge of Unanimity, No 102, in North Walsham, Norfolk has a ritual which is recognisably derived from that of Bristol, a circumstance which is due to the fact that the Bristol wool merchants who traded in North Walsham in the eighteenth century, and eventually settled there, brought their ritual with them and established it there.

Grand Lodge has rarely attempted to exert any influence on ritual matters, although its tacit acceptance of printed rituals has probably contributed more to a standardisation of ritual than any other factor. It has not, however, been to a common standard. The booklist of Lewis Masonic publishers contains a dozen different rituals, and there are more. In many cases the differences are minor, in some extensive. Nor do all Lodges follow a printed ritual, many preferring to adhere to the traditions of their Lodges. Indeed, even when Lodges do follow one particular working, there are many who proudly follow their own customs in matters of minor detail.

The most notable intervention from Grand Lodge, was with the objective of settling upon a form of ritual which would be acceptable to two parties with conflicting ritual practice. This occurred immediately after the Union of the two rival Grand Lodges in 1813 when a special Lodge, the Lodge of Reconciliation, set to work to formulate a standard ritual procedure. The latter was demonstrated to Grand Lodge and approved, and was then demonstrated a number of times to representatives from private Lodges. In this environment a series of Lodges of Instruction sprang up, amongst them those of Stability and Emulation, each of which has a tradition of handing down unchanged the ritual forms which had been formulated by the Lodge of Reconciliation. It should be pointed out, however, that the method of instruction then was by cathechistic form rather than by a rehearsal, as it is today. While the answers to the questions described the ceremonies in some detail, it could not cover every minor point and there was enough room for differences to arise.

Later, with the arrival of printed rituals, the major established workings, particularly those of London, were put on public record and the differences became permanent. There were also attempts to improve on the existing published rituals by rewriting them. Thus, in 1936 Dr Cartwright published *The English Ritual* which was an attempt to produce a ritual which not only eliminated faults, but also corrected some of the grammatical errors which appeared in many published rituals.

Some of the many printed rituals today are:

Standard (or *Stability*)
Emulation

Taylor's
Universal
Logic
West End
Oxford
Sussex

Taylor's, *West End*, *Logic* and *Universal* are used mainly in London and its vicinity. *Taylor's* ritual was first published as the *North London Working*, but when Hill, the original publisher, died his foreman printer, Taylor, reissued it without any title and it became known simply by the latter's imprint. *Emulation* is probably the most frequently used ritual in the Home Counties.

The *Bristol* ritual has never been printed, existing only in manuscript form. It is one of the oldest workings in England, and unique in its dramatic presentation of the ceremony. Other old and individual workings include those of *Exeter* and *Humber*.

Returning to Grand Lodge intervention in ritual matters, there have been two such occasions this century. Grand Lodge almost intervened in 1926 when the Board of General Purposes submitted to Grand Lodge a report which declared certain extended working in the Installation ceremony to be irregular. Had the report been accepted and confirmed, the Lodges which used that working would have been debarred from doing so. At the September 1926 meeting of Grand Lodge the motion was carried, but following a deputation to the President of the Board of General Purposes, the December meeting effectively overturned the motion.

On another occasion, in 1964, Grand Lodge adopted permissive variations to the penalties but left it to individual Lodges to decide whether they would use the permissive form, or continue as before.

MASONIC DINNERS

As might be expected, there is much variation in these proceedings; not only from one part of the country to another, but also from one Lodge to another. The following is intended as no more than an attempt to give the flavour of the proceedings at the Masonic dinner which follows a Lodge meeting.

Frequently entitled the Festive Board, these are far more complicated than appears at first sight, and one often hears comments to the effect that more attention should be given it at Lodges of Instruction. The 'work' is mainly in the hands of the Master, Immediate Past Master or Director of Ceremonies (depending on Provincial or Lodge tradition), and to a minor extent the Wardens, while the Stewards carry out their duties at table.

Preparation for each Masonic dinner usually begins at the meeting of the Lodge committee prior to the Lodge meeting itself, when members are assigned to toast the visitors, the Past Masters and Officers of the Lodge, etc. Replies, eg from a visitor, are also arranged in advance when possible.

The seating at the dinner is arranged in such a way that the Master is flanked on his left by the Immediate Past Master and, in order of seniority, the other Officers of the Lodge; and on his right by the Initiate if there is one and, in order of seniority, the Officers representing Grand Lodge or the Province, followed by other Grand or Provincial Grand Officers.

The sequence of toasts is laid out in Provincial Year Books or information sheets, together with the names of those to be toasted. Decorations such as OBE, TD, etc are not announced as part of a toast. The first toast is the loyal toast, that to the Queen and the Craft. This is followed by a toast to the Grand Master. The Master may then permit smoking, but again local custom may dictate otherwise. For example, in Somerset this follows the toast to Grand Lodge. The next toast is to the Pro Grand Master, Deputy Grand Master, Assistant Grand Master, and Grand Officers, Present and Past. In the Provinces, this would be followed by a toast to the Provincial Grand Master, and a toast to his Provincial Grand Officers. In London, the toast would be to Holders of London Grand Rank.

The next toast, to the Worshipful Master, is given by the IPM. At Installation dinners this may be followed by the Master's Song, and a toast by the Master to the Installing Master. In some Provinces, the toast to the Master is given only at Installation dinners.

The Master next announces the toast to the Initiate, if there is one, absent brethren (traditionally as close to 9 pm as possible), visitors, and Past Masters and Officers of the Lodge. Toasts are usually followed by fire (see next section) and, if previously arranged, replies by those toasted.

Another tradition is 'taking wine' in which the Master takes wine with individuals or groups present at the dinner, eg Grand or Provincial Grand Officers, the Lodge Officers, or a Past Master who may have conducted one of the ceremonies. Wine-taking usually proceeds in order of seniority ie starting with say, the Grand Officers present. The IPM (or DC) announces each such occasion.

The Wardens provide support to the Master by following his knocks as they do in Lodge, reporting on the work of the Stewards before any wine is taken, and assisting in the Master's Song at Installation dinners.

The final event at a Masonic dinner is the Tyler's Toast which is announced by the Master, by issuing two sharp knocks.

FIRE

This is a custom peculiar to masonic dinners as an accompaniment to toasting. Each fire is preceded by the formula 'point left right' three times to give the timing, and a count of one, two, three (except that the third count consists of a clap instead of the word). Then follows the 'three times three'. In some provinces the timing is moderate, in others such as Hertfordshire, quite fast. Some Provinces vary the 'three times three'.

In many museums and collections at masonic centres, firing glasses are to be seen. These are small glasses with sturdy, rounded bottoms which would not shatter upon being banged on the table.

The earliest description in English of the practice of firing appears in the exposure *Jachin and Boaz* published in 1762. It mentions the concerted motion of replacing the glasses on the table, following which the 'three times three' is given.

A French exposure of 1742, *Le Secret des Francs-Macons* also refers to the force with which the glasses are returned to the table, 'hard enough to shatter any but the strongest vessels'. In the same exposure the glasses are referred to as Cannon, their filling as Charging, and the drinking of their contents as Grand Fire.

It is likely that Masonic fire in England was taken as a custom from the gunnery allusions contained in the French exposures which appeared here in translation. However, musket fire as an accompaniment to important toasts did occur at guild and civic functions in England in the seventeenth century, and the custom may well have originated there.

GOVERNMENT

LODGE COMMITTEES

Rule 154 of the *Book of Constitutions* states that, if authorised by its by-laws, a Lodge may appoint a Committee of its members for the purpose of considering and reporting to the Lodge proposals concerning membership and other matters. In keeping with the wording employed by this rule, or possibly following the title given to the body which controls the finances and administration of Grand Lodge (the Board of General Purposes), the Lodge committees of private Lodges are often referred to as General Purposes Committees. They are also known as Standing Committees.

A Lodge Committee has no executive powers since all proposals are decided in open Lodge by a show of hands or a ballot. In practice, the Lodge Committee does influence matters, either because many proposals are the final outcome of much previous discussion and selection of alternative options, or because the Lodge membership may be content to vote in favour of any proposal resulting from a Committee decision.

Rule 154 also decrees that the Master is entitled to preside over every Committee of the Lodge. A typical Lodge Committee consists of the Master, Wardens, Past Masters of and in the Lodge, Treasurer, Secretary, and one or two lay brethren who are elected annually. Generally it meets prior to each Lodge meeting to discuss the business of the meeting, interview prospective candidates for Initiation, and consider and discuss reports from the Secretary, Treasurer, Almoner, and Charity Steward.

It would consider the list of those waiting to be initiated, passed and raised. It would take into consideration the Master's preference for the degree he would be performing, and select as fairly as possible those to be candidates at the forthcoming meeting.

Candidates for Initiation are interviewed to determine

whether they are suitable but also to discover whether their domestic or business lives would be disrupted in any way by their attendance at Masonic meetings and Lodge of Instruction.

In considering the reports of the Secretary, Treasurer, etc the Lodge Committee are, in effect, reviewing and directing the administration and finances of the Lodge on behalf of the Lodge members.

PROVINCIAL GRAND LODGE

There are 47 Provinces, and abroad there are 35 Districts, under the Constitution of the United Grand Lodge of England. Each of these is governed by a Provincial or District Grand Master, who has jurisdiction over all the Lodges in his Province or District. Because of their greater distance from the administrative centre of Grand Lodge, Districts have slightly more autonomy but in most respects they are governed in much the same way as Provinces.

A Provincial Grand Master provides control and leadership in his Province: he has the right to summon the Officers of a Lodge, to investigate the books and papers of a Lodge, to admonish or suspend a Lodge; he may establish a local fund for Charitable purposes; and he acts as fund-raiser-in-chief by setting targets and encouraging the members in the Province to contribute towards meeting the targets. Another important function exercised by the Provincial Grand Master and his Deputy and Assistant(s), consists of generating and maintaining loyalty and Provincial unity by personal attendances at the meetings of Lodges in the Province.

There is a close relationship between a Provincial Grand Master and the Lodges under his control, which may often be seen in the way that Lodges are prepared to honour his wishes. Frequently, a Provincial Grand Master will lead by stating his views on a given subject and expressing the hope that the Lodges in his Province will see fit to abide by them.

Personalities vary, however, and there have also been examples of autocratic rule by Provincial Grand Masters who dictate in no uncertain terms, even on matters of ritual.

Much of the administration is performed by the Provincial Grand Secretary who is concerned with the membership returns, handling queries and problems from Lodge Secretaries, ensuring that all Lodges are circulated with details of Grand Lodge or Provincial Grand Lodge decisions, liaising with the Grand Secretary, and looking after general administration such as the issue of dispensations and the production of a Year Book.

Provincial Grand Lodge, which is composed of all past and present Provincial Grand Officers and the Past Masters, Masters and Wardens of Lodges in the Province meets once a year. The appointment and investiture of Provincial Grand Officers (including promotions) occupy the major part of this meeting, but reports and resolutions are nevertheless passed by those present. These include the Provincial Grand Treasurer's report, amendments to the by-laws of the Province, etc. The meeting also provides an opportunity for bringing all those present up to date on developments within the Province.

GRAND LODGE

The United Grand Lodge of England and Wales has over 8,000 lodges on its register with a membership which is estimated as being in excess of half-a-million. The control of this vast and spread-out membership is achieved by central as well as regional government. The regional authority is located in the Provincial and District Grand Masters who lead and control those under their jurisdiction. Central government is mainly in the hands of the Board of General Purposes which, however, acts very much as a policy forming body, relying on six Committees for the detailed work. They are:

1. Finance Committee which is responsible for controlling the expenditure of the income from the Fund of General Purposes which includes fees for warrants, contributions from Lodges, rents received for use of Lodge rooms, etc. The expenditure covers rates, electricity, heating, maintenance, office staff, etc as well as payments to the Fund of Benevolence, which makes contributions to Masonic and other charities.
2. External Relations Committee which is concerned with the recognition of other Grand Lodges and the relationship with them.
3. Procedure Committee which is responsible for determining correct procedure, where interpretation is required, in accordance with the Constitutions. Ritual matters are, as in the Constitutions, excluded.
4. Premises Committee which handles the properties of Grand Lodge including Freemasons' Hall.
5. Staff Committee which deals with the clerical staff and matters related to personnel, pay, pensions, etc.
6. Library, Art and Publications Committee which is concerned with the work of the Library and Museum, and the publications issued by Grand Lodge such as the Year Book.

The Board of General Purposes meets eight times a year to consider the various reports and to determine policy as necessary.

At each quarterly meeting of Grand Lodge, a report of the Board of General Purposes is read to those attending, who then vote for its adoption. The Report is entered on the Minutes and by means of the Extracts from the Proceedings, is circulated to all Lodges. Following the adoption of the Report of the Board, Grand Lodge votes on any individual recommendations contained in the Report, such as amendments to the rules in the *Book of Constitutions*, giving recognition to an overseas Grand Lodge, erasures of Lodges, etc. The voters in this democracy are those attending the particular meeting at which the proposals are made. Entitlement to attend Grand Lodge is given to any Grand Officer, past or present (except Past Grand Stewards unless they qualify under another heading), and Past Masters, Masters and Wardens of private Lodges.

Proposals do not only originate with the Board of General Purposes: they may also be made, following a notice of motion, by Grand Lodge members. An example of such a 'private bill' occurred in 1964 when following a Paper on *The Masonic Penalties* in the Quatuor Coronati Lodge in 1963, the Provincial Grand Master for Norfolk proposed a permissive variation to the penalty in each of the three degrees. The proposal had been preceded by six months of widespread discussion so that the December 1964 meeting of Grand Lodge was attended by greater numbers than usual. Voting was overwhelmingly in favour of the proposal and thus the permissive variations were adopted.

There are also decisions which are not influenced by Grand Lodge at all, but are in the hands of the Grand Master alone. The powers of the Grand Master are laid out in the *Book of Constitutions* and include that of forming or re-arranging Provinces or Districts, appointing Provincial and District Grand Masters, and appointing certain members of the Board of General Purposes.

In addition to the work of government, there is a great deal of administration to be done. Much of this is carried out by the Grand Secretary and his staff, who are concerned on a full-time basis with exercising the day-to-day control of matters related to nearly 1,700 London Lodges, and being involved in the administration of well over 6,000 Lodges in the Provinces and Districts.

THE CHARITIES

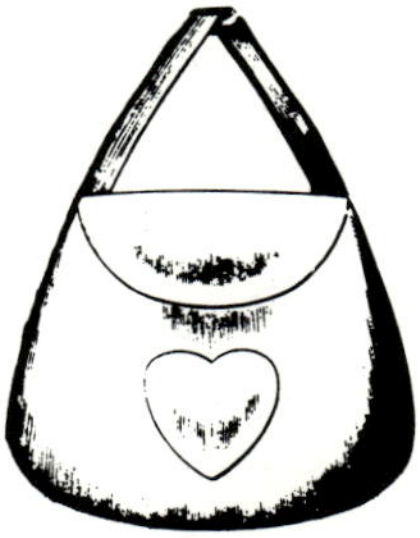

FUND OF BENEVOLENCE

An early consequence of the formation of Grand Lodge in 1717 was the appointment of a Committee of Charity. From 1729, a General Fund of Charity began to receive on a regular basis, contributions and donations from Lodges registered under the new Grand Lodge. When the Antients Grand Lodge was formed, they too set up a charitable fund and formed, in 1754, the Committee of Charity. The first *Book of Constitutions* to be published after the Union of the two Grand Lodges, specified a Committee of Benevolence to administer charity under the supervision of Grand Lodge. The fund which provided for such relief received its income from quarterages and other fees.

In recent years, the method of contribution to the Fund of Benevolence has changed to one of capitation whereby each member of a Lodge pays, as part of his Grand Lodge dues, a contribution towards the Fund. The Fund was until 31 December 1980, administered by the Board of Benevolence who considered, in the main, petitions for assistance from members of the Craft, their widows and their children under the age of 21 years, and supplied relief as necessary.

Since 1981 the equivalent role (but with substantially broader powers) has been exercised by Grand Charity and the Fund of Benevolence has been transferred to the control of the Grand Charity. Contribution by capitation remains but the contributions have been increased by extending the Festival system to include the Grand Charity (see Bagnall Report, and Festivals).

THE ROYAL MASONIC INSTITUTION FOR GIRLS

This institution started life as The Royal Cumberland Free Masons' School in 1788, 'for the maintenance and education of female orphans and distressed female children of indigent brethren of Free and Accepted Masons under the protection of Her Royal Highness the Duchess of Cumberland'. It was founded, under the Premier Grand Lodge, largely through the initiative of Bartholomew Ruspini. The latter was a surgeon who specialised in dentistry and became the King's dental surgeon. He was an eminent figure in London society and connected with a great many London Lodges.

The first 15 girls were admitted in 1789 at the original premises near today's Euston Station. From there the School moved several times, including a long stay at Wandsworth Common, until the present School was opened in 1934 at Rickmansworth Park, Hertfordshire. Set in 316 acres of parkland, the School sets out not only to educate those daughters of Freemasons who are bereft of the care of one or both parents, but also to provide them with the personal attention which they would have received from their own parents.

The School is thus delivering, at the end, stable and complete individuals (who are able to make their own contributions to society) rather than simply caring for their physical needs.

Girls at the School are provided with clothing, school books and materials; examination fees are paid; and generally the School accepts full parental responsibility.

When the Bagnall Report was issued in 1973, there were 426 girls at the School (including 99 fee paying girls), and a further 430 were being supported at other schools. The School also provides grants for higher education and training.

The RMIG is administered from 31 Great Queen Street, London WC2B 5AG.

THE ROYAL MASONIC INSTITUTION FOR BOYS

In 1798 a second charity was established with a view to caring for the children of indigent Freemasons. It was initiated by a Lodge under the Antients, and had the purpose of clothing and educating the sons of indigent Freemasons without, however, creating a school to do so. Ten years later a similar charity was founded under the Moderns. The two Charities were amalgamated in 1817 following the Union of the two Grand Lodges.

In 1857 the first school was opened in North London at Wood Green, to be followed in 1903 by a larger school at Bushey in Hertfordshire. The school was eventually closed after 120 years of existence following the recommendations of the Bagnall Report, but the RMIB continues in its original objective of caring for the sons of Freemasons. Boys are sent to boarding or day schools with the fees and costs being met by the RMIB. There is also a system of care and supervision whereby boys are sponsored by individual Lodges who nominate specific members to maintain a watching brief over each boy, providing attention and guidance until he reaches adulthood, or even later if necessary.

The RMIB is administered from 26 Great Queen Street, London WC2B 5AG.

THE ROYAL MASONIC BENEVOLENT INSTITUTION

The RMBI came into existence in 1850, by the amalgamation of an 'Asylum for Aged and Decayed Freemasons' (which charity erected a building in Croydon to house 50 annuitants), and a Masonic Benevolent Annuity Fund which also extended to widows.

Accommodation was a secondary object, and it was not until 1955 that the Croydon establishment was sold and the first in a series of modern Homes built at Hove, Sussex. Since then, Homes have been opened in several places including York, Berkshire and South Wales. These Homes are really modern flats with ancillary nursing units.

The primary objects of the RMBI for many years, however, was the payment of annuities to aged Freemasons and their dependants. Such annuities are quite small and are only extended to those who are truly in need and have been paid-up members of a Lodge for at least 15 years. Today, the RMBI has a two-fold objective which covers equally the need to provide annuities to aged Freemasons (and their dependants) who may require financial assistance, and the need to provide accommodation in Residential Homes or Nursing Homes for aged Freemasons (and dependant women) with limited financial resources, who are in need of such accommodation.

The RMBI is administered from offices at 20 Great Queen Street, London WC2B 5AG.

THE ROYAL MASONIC HOSPITAL

The plan for the establishment of a Hospital and Nursing Home was first aired in 1911. It received Grand Lodge approval in 1913. The outbreak of the First World War in 1914 delayed the original scheme, but gave rise to the maintenance of nursing homes for wounded soldiers. In 1920 the old Chelsea Women's Hospital in Fulham Road, West London was opened as the first Freemasons' Hospital and Nursing Home.

The 50 beds it contained soon had a long waiting list, and it became clear that larger premises were required. A large site was acquired in West London, near Ravenscourt Park, and in 1933 the present hospital was opened by King George V accompanied by Queen Mary. Later additions include a Nurses' Home, a School of Nursing, new operating theatres and pathology laboratories, an additional surgical ward, and other improvements necessary to the maintenance of a modern hospital.

Top medical consultants are employed at the Hospital to

ensure a high quality of care for its patients. The accommodation consists mainly of small 4-bedded wards and single rooms. Contributions towards treatment, etc are required from those in a position to make them, while others are subsidised by a Samaritan Fund. A very high proportion of Masonic patients are subsidised, some completely. Some 5,000 patients are admitted each year.

OTHER CHARITIES

While the foregoing are the major charities, they are not the only beneficiaries of Masonic charity.

There are, for example, fund-raising efforts towards local enterprises such as the Hertfordshire Old People's Establishment (HOPE) which has been financed entirely by that Province.

In recent years, many grants have also been made to non-Masonic charities. Reference to each December's Quarterly Communications of Grand Lodge will show the long list of welfare societies, medical research associations etc which have benefited from the Grand Charity general fund. In addition, there have been large grants for specific projects such as £300,000 in 1980 to the Royal National Lifeboat Institution for a lifeboat (subsequently named 'Duchess of Kent') and £250,000 in 1981 to the Royal Association for Disability and Rehabilitation towards a project for improving the assessment and treatment of those suffering from severe speech impairment. Another long-standing beneficiary of Masonic fund-raising is the Royal College of Surgeons which receives an income from a trust fund established to mark the 250th anniversary of Grand Lodge in 1967. In 1982 the Royal College of Surgeons reported that the accumulated total of grants from the fund to research projects in the College exceeded half-a-million pounds.

THE BAGNALL REPORT AND AFTER

A Committee of Inquiry was appointed in 1971 to consider the Charities in respect of their effectiveness and financial management, and to consider the methods adopted for fund-raising, and amongst others whether competition between the Charities was in the best interests of the Craft and of the Charities. The Chairman of the Committee was the Hon Mr Justice Bagnall.

The Committee presented its Report in December 1973, and since then has reported on progress at every December meeting of Grand Lodge. The Report covers 102 pages with a further 43 pages of Appendices. It describes the origin and the then existing situation of each of the four Charities and the Board of Benevolence, discusses their finances and legal position, organisation and administration, investments, and contains a blue-print for the future.

The recommendations were based on the view that the existing arrangements were too rigid and less than efficient in the allocation of funds and their investment profitability; that rationalisation of the Charities both in administration and as trusts would be more cost effective and provide an improved service to the Craft; and that the Craft, through the members of Grand Lodge, should have control over the allocation of charitable contributions among the Charities.

Among the recommendations were the following major proposals:

1. An amalgamation of the RMIG and the RMIB into a single Charity, the Educational Trust. This became the Masonic Trust for the Girls and Boys.
2. An amalgamation of the RMBI and the RMH into a single Charity, the Foundation for the Aged and the Sick.
3. The creation of a Central Charity (later renamed the Grand Charity) which would be a fund raising and fund distributing Charity.
4. The financing of the Central Charity by contributions, but also by an increase of the capitation fee in respect of each

Lodge member, payable as part of Grand Lodge dues to the Fund of Benevolence, the latter to be transferred to the control of the Central Charity.

Many other recommendations of a minor nature or of detail were made, in all running to a list of 60 points.

The Masonic Foundation for the Aged and Sick was constituted in 1979, the Grand Charity in 1980, and the Masonic Trust for the Girls and Boys in 1982.

The Grand Charity came into operation on the 1 January 1981. It assumed the role of the Board of Benevolence, the Fund of Benevolence having been transferred to the control of the Grand Charity on 31 December 1980. It continues the work of the Board of Benevolence, but acts also in its central role of distributing contributions 'to the objects which the Craft desires to benefit' including the Hospital, etc but also to non-Masonic Charities. It will, moreover, provide an accounting and investment service to Lodges, and 'review continuously the direction and effectiveness of Masonic charity'.

FESTIVALS

A Festival was the traditional method of collecting donations employed by three of the Masonic Charities, the RMIG, RMIB, and RMBI. The Royal Masonic Hospital has always declined the support of a Festival. The names of the Charities have changed but there are still three Festivals organised each year, one per Charity. Today these are The Masonic Trust for the Girls and Boys, The Masonic Foundation for the Aged and the Sick, and the Grand Charity.

Each Festival is sponsored by a Province, or occasionally by the Grand Secretary or Assistant Grand Master, or all the London Lodges. A Province is always more than assisted in its efforts by London Lodges and by individuals.

A Festival is the outcome of a sustained effort, over a period of seven years or more, in collecting on behalf of one of the Charities. It is capped by a celebratory dinner at which the Provincial Grand Master presides, and at which the amounts contributed by each of the Lodges in the Province and elsewhere are announced, followed by the declaration of the grand total.

During the seven years or so leading up to a Festival, the Charity collections of Lodge meetings plus convenants from Lodge members, proceeds from social evenings, etc are mainly directed towards a target set for each Lodge by the Provincial Grand Master. Co-operation towards such schemes by individual Lodges are entirely voluntary, but it would be unusual to find support for the Festival wanting.

Each of the Masonic Charities are registered as a charity, enabling it to reclaim, on covenants, the income tax paid by a contributor. Thus covenants enable the Charities to benefit, at no extra cost to the contributor, a further 43 per cent of the contribution from a person paying basic rate of tax, and correspondingly greater proportions from those paying higher rates of tax. The responsibility for explaining such advantages together with an introduction to the Masonic Charities (coupled with visits where possible) rests with the Charity Steward of each Lodge.

HISTORICAL BACKGROUND

THE AGE OF THE MASONIC TRADITION

By means of a variety of references in our ceremonies to antiquity, we may be led to suppose that Masonry dates back to biblical days, particularly to the building of King Solomon's temple. The evidence available, however, points strongly to the fact that speculative Freemasonry dates back only as far as the seventeenth century, or just possibly as far back as the reign of Elizabeth I. This evidence will be discussed shortly. Operative masonry does, of course, date further into the past, in England certainly to the period immediately following the Norman conquest in the eleventh century, when the major buildings of the Norman style were begun, such as the cathedrals and abbey churches at Canterbury, Lincoln, St Albans, Winchester and Gloucester, to name but a few. Operative masons, however, apart from their practical work, were concerned with the moral and professional behaviour of practicing craftsmen as well as matters such as rates of pay and keeping out unskilled workers.

What then does operative masonry have to do with speculative Masonry and why are our ceremonies based on the traditions and vocabulary of medieval builders? Part of the answer lies in the fact that manuscripts exist which indicates that these medieval builders had not only a set of articles and ordinances which prescribed their behaviour, but also a history of masonry which places its origins in biblical days, and which told of the approval of masonry by a variety of illustrious persons from Solomon in c950 BC to King Athelstan in the tenth century AD. A version of the articles, ordinances, and history exists today in a literary work which dates from c1390, known as the *Regius MS*. Another manuscript, the *Cooke*, containing a more extensive history, dates from c1420. From references contained in the *Cooke* Manuscript, such as those to the 'Polychronicon', a Latin history whose author died in 1364, and which was translated into English in 1387, it seems unlikely that the history was a product of a period earlier than the mid-fourteenth century. The *Regius* Manuscript gives the impression of being one of the several English literary efforts of the fourteenth century which marked the supersedure of French as the written language, in this case based on an account of the traditions of operative masons.

The medieval history and code of conduct, the latter subsequently becoming known as the Charges, were in later centuries repeated in a whole series of manuscripts numbering well over a hundred, and dating from 1583 to the nineteenth century. The later manuscripts clearly belong to speculative Masonry, several containing additional articles of a speculative nature, while the earlier seventeenth century manuscripts do not contain any internal evidence that they were necessarily other than documents used by operative masons, although there is a strong possibility that they reflect the emergence of speculative Masonry.

Certainly, the manuscript dating from 1583 and those that follow, contain two elements which foreshadow the future development of speculative Masonry. One is a statement to the effect that the history is to be read or told at the time when a Mason 'should be made, for to give him his Charge'. The second is a Latin phrase which indicates that the person being made places his hand upon a Book (probably the *Holy Bible*) while he listens to the Charges.

Quite how or why speculative Masonry arose is not clear. Explanations range from the purely social, to reasons bedded in the emergence of intellectual freedom during the Renaissance which came late to England. We have to assume that there existed an attraction to men of reason in the traditions of operative masonry. These included the charges, the legendary history, the admission rite, and possibly the recital from memory of the manuscript contents. Later, possibly in the wake of James I of England, IV of Scotland, came the traditions of Scottish operative masonry including secret modes of recognition.

The evidence relating to the existence of speculative Masonry in the seventeenth century is contained, amongst others, in the following two sources:

The earliest reference we have to an activity which may be differentiated from the practices of operative masons occurs in a 1621 account book of the London Company of Masons, a guild which had been founded in 1376 and received its Grant of Arms in 1472–73. The entry in the 1621 account book refers to 'making masons' of seven men, three of whom were already members of the Company. Later entries use the term 'accepted' or 'Acceptance', an entry in 1648 referring to someone who was already a Warden of the Company 'Coming on The Accepcon'.

The next reference is dated 1646 and is found in the diary of a man who was clearly not connected with the building trade. Elias Ashmole, who had been admitted a solicitor at the age of 21, and later founded the Asmolean museum at Oxford, as a young man of 29 wrote in his diary for October 16, 1646 that he was 'made a Freemason at Warrington in Lancashire'. He gives the names of others present, none of whom can be said to be operative masons.

There is further evidence during the seventeenth century but the above is sufficient to make the point that there was in existence, during the first half of the seventeenth century, a masonic practice which was separate from that of the operatives. The records of the London Masons' Company prior to 1621 unfortunately have not survived and we are unable to trace further back the practice of making of masons of men who were already in the Company.

What we are left with is the fact that speculative Masonry, although dating back a mere three to four centuries, is founded on traditions of operative masonry which date back to the fourteenth century. There are, of course, other possibilities but these must, until further evidence is uncovered, remain speculation.

THE OLD CHARGES

In everyday terms, the 'ancient charges' are brought to our attention by the Installation Ceremony in which the Master Elect has read to him certain Ancient Charges and Regulations printed in the *Book of Constitutions*. These ancient charges are derived from manuscript documents, commonly referred to as the Old Charges, or Manuscript Constitutions. The earliest two manuscripts date back to the late fourteenth and early fifteenth centuries, and relate to medieval operative masons.

The manuscripts usually consist of two sections. One contains a series of moral and professional charges such as 'no Master or Fellow shall take upon him any Lord's work nor any other man's work unless he knows himself able and sufficient to perform the same . . .' or, 'no Mason shall be a thief, or conceal any such unjust action, so far forth as he may wit or know'.

These charges are preceded by a legendary history which explains the origin of the charges and the beginnings of the craft of masonry in biblical days, tracing it to its development in England. The history is called 'legendary' because it bears little relation to historical fact. For example, Euclid, a noted geometrician of the third century BC, is referred to as the clerk of Abraham (approximately 2000 BC) from whom he received masonic instruction. Of particular interest is the appearance in its narration of Solomon's Temple, together with a reference to his master mason from Tyre. In later years, speculative Masonry expanded this episode during the formulation of what today is the third degree. The contents of one of the early manuscripts is given at the end of this book.

There are over 100 of the Old Charges known today. They descend from one another in the sense that each appears to have been copied from an earlier version. We do not, of course, possess all the Old Charges created, but it is possible to draw up a table of descent using similarities in the account of the legendary history, copying errors, and the introduction of new material. In this way a kind of family tree has been drawn up. This, together with actual dates of the documents, where known, has made it possible to arrange them chronologically and to trace the development of its contents. The legendary history was revised on several occasions, but in its earliest form it probably dates from the fourteenth century.

The following will give an idea of the distribution of the Old Charges over the period up to the end of the sixteenth century:

c1390	:	*Regius Poem*
c1410	:	*Cooke* Manuscript
1583	:	*Grand Lodge No 1* Manuscript
c1600	:	*Lansdowne* Manuscript

Following these, there are seven Old Charges dated to the first half of the seventeenth century, and about 40 dates to the second half of the seventeenth century.

Judged by their content, those of the sixteenth century and later were used when 'any Mason should be made'. They clearly contain an obligation in the sense of placing the hand on a Bible while the Charges are given. This practice would not have been unique to those in the mason's trade since it was common guild practice for newcomers to swear upon the Bible to observe the ordinances of the guild. Gradually, however, the Old Charges changed character as new material crept in. Some Old Charges were expanded to contain conditions on which a person may be accepted as a Freemason, and these are quite definitely related to speculative Freemasonry. One condition attaching to the entry to a Lodge stipulates the person bringing a 'Certificate of the Time and Place of his Acception'. At some stage, then, the legendary history and charges were borrowed by speculative Masonry and developed. With the exception of additional material such as the speculative conditions and revisions of the legendary history, the later Old Charges remained in the same mould as those of the earlier period, and we have to turn to other material for information on the development of speculative Masonry (see The Development of the Ceremonies).

THE DEVELOPMENT OF GRAND LODGE

The development of Grand Lodge covers three separate stages:

i The formation of the original Grand Lodge in 1717 and its subsequent existence,

ii the inception of a separate Grand Lodge in 1751 followed by a long period of rivalry between the two bodies, and

iii the union of the two Grand Lodges in 1813 and the period of expansion running up to the present time.

The premier Grand Lodge was founded by a small group of London Lodges. Unfortunately no minutes were kept until those of 1723, but it appears from the account given by Anderson in his second *Constitutions* (1738) that four Lodges meeting in ale-houses and taverns in St Paul's Church-Yard, Drury Lane, Covent Garden and Westminster, determined to form a Grand Lodge and selected from amongst themselves a Grand Master. They restricted their jurisdiction to Lodges in London and Westminster, an area of no more than a few square miles. However, they were joined by existing Lodges or themselves constituted new Lodges, for within a short period the number of Lodges associated with the new Grand Lodge had grown considerably.

In 1721 the first nobleman was chosen as Grand Master,

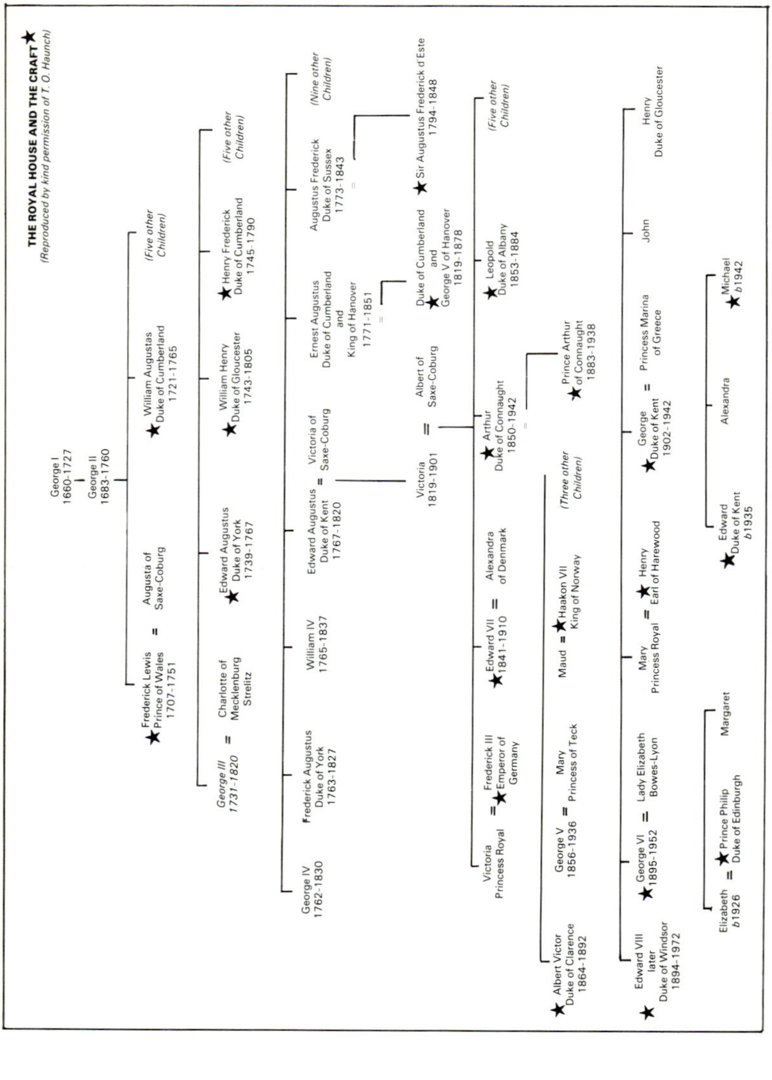
THE ROYAL HOUSE AND THE CRAFT ★
(Reproduced by kind permission of T. O. Haunch)
George I 1660-1727
George II 1683-1760
★ Frederick Lewis Prince of Wales 1707-1751
=
Augusta of Saxe-Coburg
★ William Augustas Duke of Cumberland 1721-1765
(Five other Children)
George III 1731-1820
=
Charlotte of Mecklenburg Strelitz
★ Edward Augustus Duke of York 1739-1767
★ William Henry Duke of Gloucester 1743-1805
★ Henry Frederick Duke of Cumberland 1745-1790
(Five other Children)
George IV 1762-1830
Frederick Augustus Duke of York 1763-1827
William IV 1765-1837
Edward Augustus Duke of Kent 1767-1820
=
Victoria of Saxe-Coburg
Ernest Augustus Duke of Cumberland and King of Hanover 1771-1851
Augustus Frederick Duke of Sussex 1773-1843
(Nine other Children)
Victoria 1819-1901
=
Albert of Saxe-Coburg
★ Duke of Cumberland and George V of Hanover 1819-1878
★ Sir Augustus Frederick d'Este 1794-1848
Victoria Princess Royal
=
★ Frederick III Emperor of Germany
★ Edward VII 1841-1910
=
Alexandra of Denmark
★ Arthur Duke of Connaught 1850-1942
★ Leopold Duke of Albany 1853-1884
(Five other Children)
★ Prince Arthur of Connaught 1883-1938
★ Albert Victor Duke of Clarence 1864-1892
George V 1856-1936
=
Mary Princess of Teck
Maud
=
★ Haakon VII King of Norway
(Three other Children)
★ Edward VIII later Duke of Windsor 1894-1972
★ George VI 1895-1952
=
Lady Elizabeth Bowes-Lyon
Mary Princess Royal
=
★ Henry Earl of Harewood
★ George Duke of Kent 1902-1942
=
Princess Marina of Greece
John
Henry Duke of Gloucester
Elizabeth b1926
=
★ Prince Philip Duke of Edinburgh
Margaret
★ Edward Duke of Kent b1935
Alexandra
★ Michael b1942

and the tradition of a noble or Royal occupying the office has continued ever since. Within twenty years, both Ireland and Scotland followed the example of the first Grand Lodge and constituted their own Grand Lodges.

In 1727 a committee was appointed to administer a charity fund and contributions from private Lodges began in 1729. Gradually, this committee had its powers enlarged until it became almost a Board of General Purposes. The first Provincial Grand Masters had been appointed by 1726. It was by no means an office of delegated authority equal to that of the present organisation, but it demonstrates the speed with which the concept of a Grand Lodge took hold in outlying areas such as Wales and Cheshire. By 1728, overseas Lodges had been constituted in Gibraltar, Madrid and Bengal.

The initial impetus, certainly at government level, died out shortly afterwards and a long period of lack-lustre administration followed. A series of Grand Masters showed little interest in their duties. Also, following Prichard's *Masonry Dissected* in 1730, an exposure which provided details of the ceremonies sufficient to alarm Grand Lodge, it was decided to implement certain variations 'in the established forms' to detect imposters. These were not popular with those who were against any innovation in Masonry. Thus the ground was prepared for the formation of a second, and rival, Grand Lodge in 1751.

It consisted initially of some 80 Masons, many of them Irish, who took care to specify both in their title and their rules, that they were an 'Ancient and Honourable Society of Free and Accepted Masons' who desired to 'revise the Ancient Craft upon true Masonical principles'. Possibly, however, they simply wanted to be free to organise themselves outside of the control of the indigenous Grand Lodge. They were assured of a place in posterity when, in the second year of their existence, they elected Laurence Dermott as Grand Secretary. In the same way that Anderson had popularised the original Grand Lodge and Masonry as a whole, Dermott employed his talents and energy to create an ascendancy for the 1751 Grand Lodge.

He produced a set of by-laws for private Lodges, and in 1756 issued the first edition of the *Constitutions* of his Grand Lodge, *Ahiman Rezon*. Seven further editions followed, the final one in 1813. Dermott is also credited with popularising the terms 'Antients' which describes the new Grand Lodge, and 'Moderns' describing the original Grand Lodge. The terms had appeared in a satire by Swift, *The Battle of the Books*, published in 1704 and on the whole Swift supports the ancients, represented by Homer, Aristotle, Plato, etc against the moderns represented by Milton, Dryden, Descartes, etc.

The Antients, as they became known, had within 20 years some 200 Lodges on their Register, which represented just under half that of the premier Grand Lodge. In 1771 the third Duke of Atholl was installed Grand Master and, except for a 10 year interval, he and his son, the fourth Duke, reigned until the Union in 1813.

Moves towards a reconciliation began during the closing years of the eighteenth century. There was some incentive from the political situation following the French Revolution, and the outbreak of war with the French, when societies requiring an oath not authorised by law were being suppressed. Freemasons' Lodges were exempted but it had been demonstrated that a united body of Freemasons would be more effective.

A Lodge of Promulgation was formed in 1809 by the original Grand Lodge to report on the differences of ritual between the Lodges of the two bodies.

In 1813 the fourth Duke of Atholl was succeeded as Grand Master of the Antients by the Duke of Kent, brother of the Duke of Sussex who was then the new Grand Master of the original Grand Lodge. The two Grand Lodges signed their Articles of Union in the same year. The Duke of Kent proposed his brother, the Duke of Sussex, as first Grand Master of the United Grand Lodge, and the latter was formally elected following the ceremony of Union on 27 December 1813.

The Duke of Sussex remained Grand Master for 30 years. Throughout the remainder of the nineteenth century, which saw only four Grand Masters, this pattern of stability was maintained, culminating in the Grand Mastership of the Prince of Wales up to his enthronement as King Edward VII in 1901. The twentieth century has provided an equally steady period beginning with the Duke of Connaught, who was Grand Master for 38 years, and apart from the war years and those immediately following, bringing us up to date with the Earl of Scarborough who was Grand Master from 1951 to 1967, and the present Grand Master, the Duke of Kent who took office in 1967.

The brief summary below gives some idea of the major events, other than those already mentioned, which occurred during the existence of Grand Lodge:

1724 Committee of Charity appointed
1776 First Freemasons' Hall in Great Queen Street
1788 Royal Masonic Institution for Girls founded
1798 Royal Masonic Institution for Boys established (by the Antients)
1837 Grand Lodge Library started
1838 Royal Masonic Benevolent Institution founded
1902 Boys' school at Bushey completed
1913 Grand Lodge approves the opening of Masonic Nursing Homes, the predecessors to the Masonic Hospital
1933 Present Freemasons' Hall opened
1933 Royal Masonic Hospital opened
1934 Girls' school at Rickmansworth opened

The growth of Freemasonry under the United Grand Lodge can be seen from the following table, which shows the number of Lodges constituted during each of the following periods:

by 1820	:	363
1820 to 1840	:	109
1840 to 1860	:	394
1860 to 1880	:	995
1880 to 1900	:	938
1900 to 1920	:	1,243
1920 to 1940	:	1,782
1940 to 1960	:	1,890
1960 to 1980	:	1,218

This growth was in no small measure attributable to the influence and control exercised by Grand Lodge, which enabled Masonry to retain its purity and stability.

ANDERSON'S CONSTITUTIONS *AND LATER*

Anderson's *Constitutions*, published in 1723, was the forerunner of the present *Book of Constitutions*. In it were published the first General Regulations, and while these occupied a mere 12 pages out of a total of 91, they represent the beginnings of a set of Rules which today governs the Craft.

Anderson came to London from Scotland and served as a Minister of the Church of Scotland. In 1721 he started work on a history of the Order based loosely on the material in such of the Old Charges as were known to him. The history eventually occupied some 48 pages of his Book. To this he added the General Regulations, credited to George Payne when he was Grand Master in 1720; a summary of the ancient charges; a postscript which detailed the manner of constituting a new Lodge; and several pages of songs. The General Regulations were particularly concerned with Grand Lodge and the Grand Master, but amongst the references to private Lodges one or two are to be found which are familiar to us today, for example:

But no Man can be enter'd a Brother in any particular Lodge, or

> admitted to be a Member thereof, without the unanimous Consent of all the Members of that Lodge then present when the Candidate is propos'd, . . . Nor is this inherent Privilege subject to a Dispensation; because the Members of a particular Lodge are the best Judges of it; . . .

In 1738 Anderson produced a second and enlarged *Book of Constitutions*. The History was much extended, and more fanciful, and the General Regulations had been amended. Both the old and the new form of the Regulations were given, although the new form consisted more of annotations and amendments to the original. In the above example, the Regulation had been amended to allow a Lodge 'to admit a Member, if not above 3 Ballots are against him'. However, the old form in the 1738 edition does not match precisely the text of the 1723 edition. Either Anderson was quoting from a later text, or in typical style he was not too concerned with accuracy.

Nevertheless, both editions of the *Constitutions* issued by Anderson had the approval of Grand Lodge, and had been perused by a Grand Lodge committee. No doubt they were concerned less with the History and past Regulations, than with the accurate presentation of the rules then in force.

In 1754 , another Committee was appointed to revise the 1738 *Constitutions* (Anderson had died in 1739), and the revised third edition, under the editorship of John Entick, appeared in 1756. Two more editions followed before the Union in 1813. The present *Book of Constitutions* lists the 1815 edition, ie the sixth, as the first of the principal editions to have been published under the authority of the United Grand Lodge.

The 1841 edition omitted the History and began the regular form used since. A thorough revision took place with the issue of the 1884 edition. Considerable attention had been given to the task by the Board of General Purposes, and the proposed changes were circulated in 1882 by order of Grand Lodge before being accepted to the satisfaction of all.

The present *Book of Constitutions* (1979) is almost entirely taken up with the Laws and Regulations for the Government of the Craft together with illustrations of the Jewels, Chains, Collars and Aprons of the various Offices. It is the twenty-eighth edition to have appeared since the formation of the United Grand Lodge.

THE DEVELOPMENT OF THE CEREMONIES

Charting the development of the ceremonies is an extremely difficult task due to the lack of evidence. It seems advisable, therefore, to work backwards as far as it is possible to do so, and progress our understanding from the familiar to the unfamiliar.

Printed Rituals

These are a comparatively recent innovation. For example, the Emulation Lodge of Improvement did not authorise the production of its own ritual until as late as 1969, although printed rituals had begun to find general acceptance during the closing decade of the previous century.

The earliest complete record in printed form of the three ceremonies was published in 1838 by George Claret. The ceremonies as portrayed by Claret are substantially as we know them today. In 1870 *The Perfect Ceremonies of Craft Masonry* published by A Lewis appeared. This went through several editions, before incorporating changes in 1898 which brought it closer to Emulation upon which it claimed to have been based. It became a very popular book, and several other printed rituals followed in its wake.

Lodges of Instruction

Several lodges of instruction were in existence soon after the Union in 1813, but the most famous, Stability and Emulation, were founded in 1817 and 1823 respectively. Both had a proud tradition of handing down orally an unchanged ritual, and while the purity of each body's tradition was at times hotly contested, they have each delivered to us a ritual which is essentially the same and, moreover, substantially agrees with that presented by Claret in 1838.

The Lodge of Reconciliation (1813–16)
This Lodge was appointed by the United Grand Lodge to settle the ritual procedure to be used by its Lodges. The Lodge contained an equal number of representatives from each of the former Grand Lodges. By late 1814, the ritual procedure they had formulated was being demonstrated, and final approval by Grand Lodge was obtained in 1816. We may assume that the accepted procedures were much as those portrayed by Claret and handed down by Emulation and Stability. We have less evidence, however, of the forms which were in existence in the Lodges of the two Grand Lodges during the previous century.

The Exposures of the Eighteenth Century
There were numerous exposures published during the eighteenth century. Amongst the best known are Prichard's *Masonry Dissected* of 1730, *Three Distinct Knocks* of 1760, and *J & B* of 1762.

These exposures are important in two respects: they shed light on the ritual of Lodges of the period, albeit only those from which the authors derived their material; and they contributed hugely to the standardisation of ritual. Their content became, in time, representative of a large number of Lodges. *Masonry Dissected* ran to three editions within the first two weeks of its appearance, and by the time *Three Distinct Knocks (TDK)* arrived in 1760, a further 14 editions had been brought out. *TDK* itself went to six editions before the end of the century, and its pirated offspring *J & B* ran to 30 editions during the same period.

In terms of providing information on contemporary ritual, there is evidence that the 1760s exposures do reflect the practice of Lodges of the period. This evidence resides in an annotated copy of *J & B* by a member of an Irish Lodge, one Zimmerman. In the margins of his copy he noted the differences between the ceremonies he witnessed, and that contained in the printed version. The differences are slight, tending to support the view that these exposures are representative of 'Antient' working in England. *J & B* itself, however, contains additions to its plagiarised original *(TDK)* which were in keeping with the practice of the 'Moderns'.

There also appeared in France during the 30 years preceding *TDK* and *J & B*, a whole series of exposures of French Masonic practice. These were sold in England either in French or in translation, and will also have had an influence on the development of the English ritual.

Three Distinct Knocks and *J & B*

These exposures of 1760 and 1762 contain elements of which there is no earlier evidence in English documents. The new elements include:

> A formal Opening and Closing of the Lodge (not each degree), very reminiscent of today's first degree work,
> Calling off and Calling on,
> Three separate obligations,
> Symbolical explanation of the working tools, and
> The Presentation of an Apron

The following provides a very brief outline of the ritual in *J & B*: The admission meeting starts with a short ceremony in which the candidate is conducted hoodwinked round the floor, has the hoodwink removed after he states that he desires to become a Mason of his own free will and choice, takes an obligation similar to that we use today, is taught the sign, grip and password of an EA, and is given an apron.

This ceremony is followed by a lecture (probably taken in comfort at table with refreshments) which employs a catechism, ie question and answer, to communicate the remainder of the information concerned with the degree. It includes, for example, a description of the Working Tools, which for this degree consists of the 24 inch gauge, the square, and common gavel.

The second degree includes the present-day password and an obligation and penalty similar to that of today. The sign too is the same and the catechism includes a very familiar description of the pillars.

The third degree again has the present-day password, a similar penalty and includes in its catechism the legend of Hiram Abif and the five points of fellowship.

Prichard's *Masonry Dissected*

The first edition of this exposure was published on the 20 October 1730. It is a 32 page pamphlet of which the larger part is concerned with giving an account of the ceremonies. This is given in the form of a catechism, which describes in part what happened or was learned at each of the three ceremonies. *Masonry Dissected* depicts a very rudimentary ceremony, possibly concerned only with sketching the broad outlines. Reference to a 1735 Charge to the Initiate (see Appendix) will show that certain parts of the ceremony, at least, were well developed and not in keeping with the brevity of the ceremonies described by Prichard's exposure. However, taking *Masonry Dissected* as it stands, it does provide us with an insight into some of the features of the ritual of the period:

- i Three degrees were worked
- ii The 'Enter'd 'Prentice's Degree' contains an obligation which, while shorter, contains the major elements of today's first degree obligation.
- iii The 'Fellow-Craft's Degree' contains references to the Temple, the Pillars, the letter G, etc but not a separate obligation.
- iv The 'Master's Degree' contains much of the Hiram legend but almost no description of the ceremony itself.

Earlier Eighteenth Century Documents

There are 16 other surviving documents, dating from 1696 to

1730, which contain catechisms and descriptions of Lodge work. Six of these appeared in print in newspapers or as pamphlets. The remainder are manuscripts, some a mere page or two in length. Some of these portray events in Scotland, and probably do not reflect contemporary practices in England, while others may represent procedure in different parts of the country. It is worth remembering that Masonry was not organised until the advent of Grand Lodge, and then only gradually. Different practices existed in different parts and there was no reason, other than that of following fashion, for uniformity in Masonic custom. New developments in some areas co-existed with unchanged practices in others.

The documents mentioned above may be consulted in *The Early Masonic Catechisms* by Knoop, Jones and Hamer (see Recommended Books). Most of them contain a description of versions of the five points of fellowship. All of them provide some information related to the procedure of admission to a Lodge.

Other references to ritual include the following:

The *Trinity College Dublin*, Manuscript dated 1711 indicates three classes of mason, ie 'Enterprentice', 'fellow craftsman', and 'Master', each with a different token and word.

The earliest reference to a raising occurs in the *Graham* MS of 1726, and includes mention of substituted secrets. The grave, however, was not that of Hiram but of Noah.

The earliest mention of Hiram's grave occurs in the *Wilkinson* MS of c1727.

Q What is the form of your Lodge
A An Oblong Square
Q Why so
A the Manner of our Great Master Hirams grave

The Old Charges

And so we are back at the Old Charges as our only lead to

what took place, in a ritual sense, in the seventeenth century. One circumstantial piece of evidence points strongly to the fact that these manuscripts were used during ceremonies at which Masons were made: the *Sloane 3848* MS is dated 16 October 1646 and inscribed as having been written by an Edward Sankey. On that day, at Warrington, Ashmole was initiated and one of those 'of the Lodge' was Mr Richard Sankey, a Warrington landowner, who had a son named Edward. It is possible to conclude, from the foregoing, that the Old Charges were copied to provide versions to be used at actual ceremonies, and that as the practice spread, an increasing number of copies were required. Indeed, by 1722 the first printed version (Roberts) probably provided the answer to a greater demand brought about by a growing number of Lodges.

Quite what form these ceremonies took we do not know. Perhaps the best answer is to quote from the *Grand Lodge No 1* MS of c1583:

> And he made a booke thereof howe the Craft was founde, and he himself bade and commanded that yt should be redd or told when any Masson should be made, and for to give him his Chardges.

EDUCATION

RECOMMENDED BOOKS

Several books have already been mentioned in earlier sections. These apart, the books below are recommended reading. Many are available from masonic booksellers; some will need to be consulted at libraries, or obtained from a specialist secondhand bookshop.

Freemasons' Hall – Sir James Stubbs and T. O. Haunch
This is a new and very attractive book on Freemasons' Hall by authors who have worked in the building for many years and know it well. Sir James Stubbs was Grand Secretary from 1958 to 1980, and T. O. Haunch retired as Grand Lodge Librarian and Curator in 1983. Colour photographs provide a vivid impression of the various sights of the building, and the text is both informative and readable.

Freemasons' Guide & Compendium – B. E. Jones
A book to be dipped into rather than read continuously. Each point, and the selection is wide and thorough, is argued in detail so that the casual reader may find himself immersed in too much detail, unable to obtain a clear picture. It is, however, a standard reference book which covers the origins and development of Freemasonry, the development of the Degrees, and provides an extensive discussion of the Lodge and matters relating to the Lodge. The Royal Arch and Mark Masonry also receive considerable attention.

The Freemason at Work – H. Carr
This collection of 200 questions and answers is both very readable and informative. It touches on a great variety of expressions which are commonly encountered but not always clear to us; explains the background to many masonic customs; and is particularly useful in placing the topics in their historical context. Also included is a paper on the Evolution of the Installation Ceremony and Ritual.

The Freemason's Pocket Reference Book – Pick and Knight, revised by F. Smyth
This small encyclopedia of nearly 400 pages makes fascinating reading. It is most valuable, however in providing a quick answer to a sudden query. As a reference work it has been enhanced by the addition of an index which provides a means of looking up subjects which are covered under another heading.

Symbolism in Craft Freemasonry – C. F. W. Dyer
Symbolism is a subject where one has to tread warily; too often interpretations are the result of a fertile imagination, rather than actual evidence.

This book does not fall into that trap. The author has combined a review of the thoughts of other writers with a critical approach to the subject. The symbolism discussed includes that of the Ornaments of the Lodge, Darkness and Light, Masonic clothing and Working Tools.

The Pocket History of Freemasonry – Pick and Knight revised 1983 by Frederick Smyth
In about 130 pages, this little book gives a very readable account of the origin and development of Freemasonry. The remaining 180 or so pages cover Freemasonry in other countries, and describe other Orders including the Royal Arch, Mark, and Ark Mariner. The historical account progresses by picking out topics and discussing each briefly so that it consists of a series of highlights which do, however, cover a great deal of ground.

The Genesis of Freemasonry – Knoop & Jones
This book is sub-titled 'An account of the rise and development of Freemasonry in its operative, accepted, and early speculative phases', which is a clear summary of its contents. The authors start their account with the medieval builders and continue it up to 1730. It is not a shallow overview but is quite obviously based on extensive research and thorough

sifting of archives for material. Any conclusion is preceded by a statement and discussion of the various possibilities, which also makes the volume a valuable summary of then (1946) available evidence. The contents include chapters on the Old Charges, the Origins of Masonic Ceremonies, and the Development of Craft Working amongst others. The work was reprinted in 1978 by the Quatuor Coronati Correspondence Circle.

History of Freemasonry – R. F. Gould
This is a classic, written in the 1880s, which has been reissued on several occasions, notably in 1951 by Herbert Poole with the latter's own valuable contribution on the Old Charges. It appeared originally as three volumes and has since been published as six volumes, four volumes and even as a Concise History in one volume. It can be heavy reading but it set a standard for accuracy of information and objective evaluation of facts. In the book Gould examined the various theories on the origin of Freemasonry, covers the development of Freemasonry in the eighteenth and nineteenth centuries, and describes the origins of Freemasonry in countries throughout the world.

The Early Masonic Catechisms – Knoop, Jones & Hamer
The contents of this volume is a banquet to the Masonic student. It contains, amongst many others, the *Edinburgh Register House* Manuscript of 1696 which gives the earliest description of a Masonic ceremony (albeit a Scottish one); the *Trinity College, Dublin* Manuscript, presumed to be of 1711, which is the earliest known document to mention three classes of mason each with its own secrets; and Prichard's *Masonry Dissected*, the famous exposure of 1730, which contained details of the three degrees including the obligation of the first, and an account of the death of Hiram Abif. Equally valuable is a long Introduction by the editors which provides excellent background to the Catechisms themselves.

Early Masonic Pamphlets – Knoop, Jones & Hamer
This is a collection of pamphlets, extracts from publications, newspaper articles, and advertisements which appeared during the period 1638 to 1735. The scarcity of material which throw light on the early days of Freemasonry, makes this a most interesting source of comment. It should be remembered, however, that much of the comment originated from uninformed writers. The contents include the extract from Plot's *Natural History of Staffordshire* (1686) which provides a brief but early abstract of an Old Charge; the *Roberts and Cole Constitutions* (1722 and 1728 respectively), two more Old Charges; and extracts from the memoirs of Elias Ashmole which gives details of his initiation in 1646 and attendance at a meeting held in London in 1682. There is also a useful Introduction by the editors.

The Early French Exposures – Edited by H. Carr
This volume includes translations of 12 French exposures which appeared during the period 1737 to 1751. They are important in giving us information on what may have been taking place in the development of the ritual during the long gap between similar publications in England: Prichard's *Masonry Dissected* in 1730, and *Three Distinct Knocks* in 1760.

Anderson's Constitutions
This facsimile edition of Anderson's 1723 and 1738 *Constitutions* has been produced as a single volume. The two *Constitutions* had previously been printed in facsimile form, the 1738 edition in 1890 with an introduction by W. J. Hughan, and the 1723 edition in 1923 with an analysis by Lionel Vibert. The value of the present edition has been much enhanced by the inclusion, unchanged, of these introductions.

Grand Lodge 1717–1967
This is the official history of Grand Lodge published by Grand Lodge itself. It contains five main sections, each written by an authority in the field. The sections are:

Freemasonry before Grand Lodge by H. Carr
The Formation 1717 to 1751 by T. O. Haunch
The Formation 1751 to 1813 by J. R. Clarke
The Union and After, 1813 to 1917 by P. R. James
The Last Fifty Years by Sir James Stubbs

There are also five Appendices with interesting subject matter.

Elementary Guide for Masonic Librarians – A. R. Hewitt
This has been included chiefly because it contains a Reading List of important Masonic books. A. R. Hewitt is, of course, the man who created the classification system which is used by the Grand Library and this volume is therefore of special interest for that reason.

Rule and Teach – Lewis Edwards
This book is subtitled 'A Practical Handbook of Masonic Law and Custom'. It describes the powers of Grand Lodge and Provincial Grand Lodge; the duties and rights of Lodges, of a Freemason, etc; and covers many points of procedure including those concerned with the conduct of the business of a Lodge, the qualifications of a candidate, and the formation of a new Lodge, to quote but a few.

BOOK OF CONSTITUTIONS

This volume is almost totally taken up by the General Laws and Regulations for the Government of the Craft. Being rules, they are phrased carefully and comprehensively which does not make them conducive to light reading. However, only a third of its pages relates to Private Lodges and once these are consulted on a specific query, the rules are found to be quite clear and concise. A full index, as well as marginal headings make it a reference book which is both easy and quick to use.

The rules are laid out in sections, each of which cover a particular aspect. Thus rules 94–98 are concerned with the constitution of a new Lodge, rules 122–127 with visiting of Lodges, and rules 132–135 with Lodges of Instruction, to mention but a few areas.

The official description of regalia, contained in rules 239–268, is accompanied by 60 illustrations of emblems of office, collars, chains, aprons and jewels.

The rules also cover Grand Lodge, the Board of General Purposes, Provincial Grand Lodge, etc and generally constitute an unambiguous and extensive source of information on all matters concerned with Masonic policy.

PROVINCIAL YEAR BOOKS

These cover all Masonic activity in a Province, and are most useful as an aid to finding out when and where meetings, including those of other Orders, are held. Many also contain the name and address of the Scribe E, Recorder, Secretary, or Registrar of each of the Lodges, Chapters, Preceptories, etc.

In terms of the Craft, the Year Books are packed with useful information. They will probably be familiar to those reading this, but it is nevertheless worthwhile pointing out some of the features which may be overlooked. These typically include:

A recommended Toast List for use at a Masonic Dinner.

A calendar showing the meeting dates of all Lodges (and Chapters, Preceptories, etc) in the Province including those of Provincial Grand Lodge, Provincial Grand Chapter, etc.

Notes on procedure: These notes generally contain practical and very useful guidance on Lodge procedure.

Addresses by the Provincial Grand Master and Provincial Grand Secretary, and a Charity Report. These are usually copies of actual addresses given at Provincial Grand Lodge meetings, and serve to communicate to the members of Lodges in the Province the progress of national and local fund-raising, the state of membership, and any guidelines that the Provincial Grand Master may wish to provide.

Details of Grand Officers in the Province, together with the Provincial Grand Officers acting and past.

Details of the Masonic Charities.

The accounts of the Provincial Grand Lodge.

For every Lodge in the Province: the Officers and Past Masters, plus other details such as number of members, meeting dates and place, and date of warrant (ie when it was founded).

A roll of subscribing membership is often included. This lists alphabetically all Masons in the Province and shows the numbers of the Lodges, Chapters, etc to which each belongs.

ENQUIRIES OFFICE, FREEMASONS' HALL

The following are some of the books and material available from this office:

Bagnall Report: A committee of enquiry into the Charities presented this 165 page report to the Grand Master in 1973. It covers the origins and development of the Masonic Charities, their financial and legal position, their administration, costs and investments, and proposals for re-organisation. The major proposals were implemented gradually over several years. Their progress is to be found in the annual reports in the December Proceedings of Grand Lodge.

Year Book: This covers both Grand Lodge and Grand Chapter. It contains various lists including numerical and alphabetical lists of Lodges and Chapters; Grand Officers; Towns where Lodges meet; Statistics on number of Lodges, Chapters and Certificates issued each year for the last ten years; and many other details.

Book of Constitutions: Every Mason will have one, but it is well worth obtaining each new issue as out-of-date copies are often misleading in that they do not contain the amendments to Rules which are made each year. These amendments are mainly made to bring rules into keeping with changing conditions.

Historical Supplement to the Year Book: This 600 page book, together with an Addendum, covers Grand Lodge from 1717 to 1976, and Grand Chapter from 1766 to 1796. It consists mainly of details of all Grand Officers during those periods showing, by rank, the Officers appointed each year.

Freemasons' Hall: An attractive book which describes, with coloured photographs, the present building and its contents.

Information for the Guidance of Members of the Craft: This booklet is a valuable adjunct to the *Book of Constitutions*. Its main contents are points of procedure in the form of recommendations adopted by Grand Lodge and decisions taken by the Board of General Purposes. The latter often rest on interpretation of the *Book of Constitutions*. For example, to the question 'Is a Master entitled to decide what procedure shall be practised during his year in office?', the reply is given: 'Rule 155 B of C lays it down that the majority of a Lodge shall regulate the proceedings.'

Grand Lodge Proceedings: The full Quarterly Communications are available on subscription. An initial payment covers the most recent Proceedings and those for the following three years. These Proceedings are mainly interesting for the reports of the Board of General Purposes, the Grand Charity, and amendments to the Rules in the *Book of Constitutions*. Extracts of these Proceedings are, of course, handed out at Lodge meetings.

A miscellany of Circulars from the Grand Secretary's Office are available free on demand. They cover topics that require clarification such as Freemasonry and the Roman Catholic Church, Lodge Charity Stewards, etc.

BOOKSELLERS AND PUBLISHERS

Lists of books, which may be purchased direct or by mail, are available from the following:

Lewis Masonic,
Terminal House,
Shepperton, Middx
TW17 8AS
Telephone: Walton-on-Thames 228950

Toye, Kenning & Spencer Limited,
19–21 Great Queen Street,
London WC2B 5B2
Telephone: 01-242 0471

Q.C. Correspondence Circle Limited,
60 Great Queen Street,
London WC2B 5AZ
Telephone: 01-405 7340

Jolly's,
2 Herbrand Street,
Russell Square,
London WC1N 1HX
Telephone: 01-237 9516

Matthews Drew & Shelbourne Limited,
60–66 Saffron Hill,
London EC1N 8QX
Telephone: 01-404 5242

The latter specialises in the literature of the non-Craft Orders.

Lewis Masonic also publish the quarterly magazine *Masonic Square*. It is available on subscription by application to the above address.

There is also an antiquarian bookseller who provides out-of-print books:

R. Gilbert,
4 Julius Road,
Bishopton,
Bristol BS7 8EU
Telephone: Bristol 46936

Note, however, that many of his prices reflect the antiquarian value of the volumes.

Suppliers of regalia will very often be able to supply the more popular rituals and books and several large bookshops such as W. & G. Foyle in Charing Cross Road, London have a masonic section.

QC CORRESPONDENCE CIRCLE

The Correspondence Circle was inaugurated in 1887 by the Quatuor Coronati Lodge which was founded by a group of nine Masonic scholars for the purpose of encouraging and co-ordinating Masonic research. The Correspondence Circle was a means of disseminating the results of research to a world-wide readership. Today, there are over 14,000 members of the Correspondence Circle, each of whom receives annually a volume containing Papers delivered in the QC Lodge or received for publication during the previous year. Membership also entitles one to attend the Lodge meetings, although not as Lodge members, and to take part in the discussions.

The Papers contained in the annual publication, entitled *Transactions* or *Ars Quatuor Coronatorum*, often represent the most recent research into their subjects. Since historical research never quite reaches a final position, or even yields enough material to reach a view, some of the Papers may appear inconclusive. However, they are without exception stimulating, and are useful in providing a fresh and critical examination of the subjects under review. Many contributors present their findings in the most minute detail and some Papers may appear daunting at first sight, but taken in broad outline at the first reading, they are soon assimilated and the detail will be useful when pursuing a specific line of enquiry.

Each volume of the Transactions contains the five Papers delivered in the Lodge during the year (including the Prestonian Lecture for the year), together with a number of other Papers. It also contains a supplement, known as the *Miscellanea Latomorum* (latomorum means 'of stone-cutters'), which consists of shorter Papers. Queries from members of the Correspondence Circle are answered in full and circulated to all members with their summonses.

Many Lodges are members of the Correspondence Circle

and receive the Transactions and summonses care of the Lodge Secretary. Individual membership is open to Master Masons. Application forms are available from The Secretary, QCCC Ltd., 60 Great Queen Street, London WC2B 5AZ.

LOCAL MASONIC RESEARCH SOCIETIES

London has the London Grand Rank Association and the Quatuor Coronati Lodge, both providing venues where more may be learnt, and where it is possible to meet others who have an interest in Masonic study.

Elsewhere, there is usually at least one Installed Masters' Lodge in each Province. At such Lodges, Talks are given and Papers presented, and many circulate their Transactions to members. The Somerset Masters' Lodge No 3746, for example, was founded in 1915 and each year still regularly produces a copy of its Transactions. Details of such a Masters' Lodge may be obtained from a Provincial Year Book, or from the office of the Provincial Grand Secretary. Being Installed Masters' Lodges, the majority do not admit Masons below the rank of Master of a Lodge. Some, such as that of Jersey, do however extend an invitation to Master Masons.

There are, in addition, Lodges of research which operate on a basis similar to that of the Quatuor Coronati Lodge. One such is the Lodge of Research No 2429 in Leicester, which was consecrated in 1892 and has a limited membership but a large correspondence circle. The latter is open to any Master Mason. It meets at Freemasons' Hall, 80 London Road, Leicester LE2 0RA, and application may be made to the Editor of the Lodge Transactions at that address. Another well-known body of research is the Manchester Association for Masonic Research. The first volume of their annual Transactions dates back to 1909–10. The Association, which has a membership in excess of 1,000, may be contacted at the Masonic Temple, Bridge Street, Manchester M3 3BT.

As at Leicester, Master Masons are accepted. There are five meetings a year with a lecture at each meeting. There is also a library of some 3,000 volumes. The Somerset Masters' Lodge No 3746 also has a Correspondence Circle which is open to Master Masons, and publishes its Transactions annually. It meets at The Masonic Hall, Bath, Somerset.

LOCAL LIBRARIES AND MUSEUMS

In addition to the large library and museum at Freemasons' Hall, Great Queen Street, libraries, museums, and displays of Masonic objects are also to be found at Provincial Grand Lodge offices, Masonic centres, and individual Lodges. The latter, in particular, often have valuable collections of objects which may have been handed down over a period of two centuries. Examples of such Lodges with fine exhibits include Amity No 137 and St Mary's No 707 in Dorset.

Provincial Grand Lodges which maintain large libraries include Cambridge, Northumberland, East Kent, Bristol and Jersey. Leicester has a library which contains in excess of 5,000 volumes plus many old records and the Transactions of their Lodge of Research. These libraries are usually advertised in the Province's Year Book. Elsewhere, the Provincial Grand Secretary will be able to direct an enquirer towards any collection of books that may exist in the Province.

There will also be Masonic centres where a collection of books, periodicals and records may be kept in a dusty corner, not maintained as a library, but nevertheless available to an interested member of a Lodge which meets there.

APPENDIX I

AN OLD CHARGE

The following is W. J. Hughan's rendering of the GRAND LODGE NO 1 MS *of 1583. The language and punctuation of the original would have made it difficult for today's reader to follow its content.*

The mighte of the Father of heaven and the wysdome of the glorious sonne through the grace and the goodness of the holy ghost that bee three persons in one God, be with us at our beginning and give us grace so to governe us here in our lyving that wee may come to his bliss that never shall have ending. Amen

Good brethren and fellowes our purpose is to tell you howe and in what manner wise this woorthy crafti of massonrie was begun and afterwards howe it was kept by woorthy Kings and Prynces & by many other worshipfull men and also to those that bee heire we will chardge ye by the chardges that longith to every free masson to keepe, for in good faithe, and they take good heed to that that is woorthy to be well kepte, for yt is a woorthy Crafte and a curious science, for their bee seavin liberall sciences of the which seavin, yt is one of them, and the names of the seavin sciences be these.

The first is Grammar and that teacheth a man to speake trewly and to write trewly. The second is Rhetoricke and that teacheth a man to speake faier in subtill terms. And the third is Dialecticke and that teacheth a man to deserne or knowe trueth from falsehoode. And the fourth is Arithmeteicke, and that teacheth a man to reken and to compt all manner of numbers. And fyfte is Geometry and that teacheth a man the mett and measure of earth and all other things. The which science is called Geometrey. And the sixth science is called Musicke, and that teacheth a man the crafte of song and voice of tongue and organe, harpe and trompe. And the seavinth science is called Astronomie, and that teacheth a man to knowe the course of the Sunne & of the Mone and of the Starrs.

These be the vii liberall Sciences, the which vii be all found by one science, that it is to saye Geometrey. And this maye a manne prove that the Science of the worlde is found by Geometrey, for Geometrey teaches a man to measure ponderation or weight of all manner of things on earthe, for there is no mann that woorketh any crafte but he woorks by some mett or by some measure. Nor no man buyeth or sellith but by some measure or some weight, and all this is Geometrey, and all these marchants and all Crafts men, and all other of the vi Sciences, and especially the ploweman and and the tillers of all manner of graine and seeds, vyneplanters and setters of other fruits, for by Grammar nor Arthmeteicke nor Astronomie nor none of all the vi Sciences can no man find mett nor measure without Geometrey. Wherfore we thinketh that the Science of Geometry is most woorthey that findeth all others.

How this woorthye Science was fyrstle begun I shall tell you. Before Noe's fludd their was a man that was called Lamech, as yt was wrytten in the Byble in the fourth chap. of genesis. And this Lamech had two wyves, the one wife height Adaa, and the other height Sella. By his first wife Adaa he gat twoe Soones, and the one heighte Jabell and the other Juball, and by the other wyfe Sella he begat a son and a daughter, and theise iiij children found the beginning of all the Crafts in the worlde. And this elder soonne Jabell found the Craft of Geometrey and he departed flocke of sheepe and lande in the field, and firste wraught houses of stone and tree (as it is noted in the chapter abovesaid.) And his brother Juball found the Craft of Musicke, Song of tongue, harp and orgain. And the third brother Tubalcain found Smights Crafte of gold, silver and copper, yron and steele. And the daughter found the Craft of Weaving.

And these Children knew well that God woulde take vengeance for synne ether by fyer or water, wherfore they wrytten their Science that they had found in ij pyllers of stone that they might be found after Noe's fludd. And the one stone was marble, for that will not burne with any fyre, and the other stone was called Latres for that would not drown in Water.

Our intent is to tell you treuly howe and in what manner these stones were found that these Sciences were wrytten in. The great Hermarines that was Cubys Sonne, the which Cubye was Semms Sonne, that was Noe's soonne. This same Hermarines was afterward called Hermes the father of Wisdome, he found one of the ij pyllers of stone and found the Science written thereon, and he taught that to other men.

And at the making of the tower of Babilon there was Massonry made muche of. And the King of Babylon that heighte Nemroth was a Masson himself and loved well the Craft as yt was said with masters of stories. And when the Citte of Nynyvie and other cities of the Est should be made, Nemroth King of Babylon sent thither fortie Massons at the request of the King of Nynyvie his cussin, and when he sent them forth he gave them a chardge in this manner. That they should be true one to another, and that they should live truely togither, and that they should serve their Lord truely for their paye so that their Master may have woorship and all that long to him, and other moe chardges he gave them and this was the first tyme that ever any Masson had any chardge of his Crafte.

Moreover when Abraham and Sara his wife went into Egypt and there taught the vij Sciences unto the Egyptians and he had a woorthy scholler that height Ewcled and he learned right well and was a Master of all the vij Sciences.

And in his daies yt befell that the Lords and the Estats of the realme had so many soonnes that they had gotten, some by their wyves and some by other ladies of the Realme, for that land ys a hot land and plenteous of genaration.

And they had no competent lyvelyhood to find their children, wherefore they made muche care. And then the Kyng of the land made a Greate Counsell and a Parliament, viz. howe might fynde their children honestly as gentlemen, and they could find no manner good wages, and then did they throughe all the realme that yf there weare any man that could enforme them that he should come unto them, and he should be so rewarded for his travell that yt should holde him well pleased. After that this cry was made then came this worthy Clarke Ewkled and said to the King and to al his great Lords, if ye will take me your children to govern and to teach them one of the vij Sciences wherewith they maye lyve honestly as gentlemen should, under a condition that you will grant me and them, that I maye have power to rule them after the manner that the Science ought to be ruled. And that the Kynge and all his Counsell granted anon, and seayled the commission. And then this woorthy tooke to him these Lordes Sonnes and taught them this Science of Geometrey in practicke for to woorke in stones all manner of woorthy woorke that longith tp buylding Churches, Temples, Castles, Towers, and Mannors and all other manner of buylding, and he gave them a chardge on this manner.

The first ys that they should be true to the Kyng and to the Lords that they serve, and that they should live well together, and be trewe every one to other, and that they sould calle every other his fellowe or els his Brother and not his servant nor his knave nor none other foule name.

And that thei should truly deserve their pay of the Lorde or the Master that they serve, and they should ordeinge the wysest of them to be Master of the woorke, and neither for love nor lynage nor riches nor favour, to sett another that has little conning to be Master of the Lordes woorke whereby the lorde should be evile served and they ashamed. And also that they should call the Governer of the woorke Master in the tyme that they woorke with him. And other many mo Chardgs that are long to tell.

And to all theise chardges he made them swear a great othe that men used in that tyme, and ordeyned for them reasonable paye that they might lyve honestly by. And also that they should come and assemble togither every yere once, howe they might woorke best to serve their Lorde for his proffitt and to their own worship, and to correct within themselves him that had trespassed against the Crafte.

And thus was the Crafte governed there. And that woorthy Clarke Ewkled gave yt the name of Geometrie, and nowe it is called through all this land Massonrey.

Sythen long after when the children of Israele weare come into the land of Behest, that is nowe called among us the Countrie of Jerusalem, King David began the Temple that is called Templi Dom, and is named with us the Temple of Jerusalem.

And this same King David loved well Massons, and cherished much, and gave them good paye, and he gave the chardges and the manners as he had learned in Egipt given by Eukled, and other chardges moe that ye shall heare afterward.

And after the deceass of the King David, Sallomon that was King Davids Soone performed out the Temple that his Father had begun. And he sent for Massons into dyvrs countries and dyvrs lands and gathered them togither, so that he had four score thousand workmen that weare workers of stone and weare all named Massons, and he chose of them three thousand that weare ordeyned to be Maisters and Governers of his woorke. And furthermore theare was a Kinge of another reigne that men calle Iram and he loved well King Sallomon and he gave him tymber to his woorke. And he had a soone that height Anyone and he was a Master of Geometrey and was chief maister of all his Massons and was Master of all his Graving and Carbing and all other manner of Massonreye that belongeth to the Temple. And this is witnessed in the Byble in the iiij of Kyngs and thirde chapter.

And the Sallomon confirmed both Chardges and Manner that his Father had given to Massons. And thus was that woorthy Crafte of Massonry confirmed in the country of Jerusalem, and in many other Kingdoms.

Curious craftes men walked about full wyde in dyvrs countries, some to learne more crafte and couninge, and some to teache them that had but little couning and so yt befell that their was a curious Masson that height Naymus Grecus that had byn at the making of Sallomon's Temple, and he came into France, and there he taught the science of Massonrey to men of France. And there was one of the Royall line of France that height Charles Martell, and he was a man that loved well suche a Crafte and drew to this Naymus Grecus and learned of him the Crafte and – upon him the Charges and the Manners. And afterwards by the grace of God he was elect to be Kyng of France.

And when he was in his estate he tooke Massons and did healp to make men Massons that weare non, and sett them to woorke, and gave them bothe the Chardge and manner and gave them good paye that he had learned of other Massons, and confirmed them a charter from yere to yere to hold their Assembly where they woulde and Cherished them right muche and thus came the Craft into France.

England in all this season stode voyde of any chardge of Massonrie untill St. Albon's tyme, and in his dayes the Kyng of England that was a pagnyn he did wall three towne aboute that is called St. Albons. And St. Albon was a woorthy Knyght and Steward to the Kyngs household and had the government of thee Realme and also of the towne walls, and loved Massons well and cherished them muche and he made their paye right good (standing as the Relme did) for gave them ijs and vid a weeke and three pence to their cheire, for before that tyme through all the Land a Mason toke but a peny a daye and his meat untill St. Albon amended yt.

And he gave them a Charter of thee Kynge and his counsell for to houlde a Generall Counsell and gave yt the name of an Assemblye, and was there at him selfe and healped for to make Massons, and gave the Chardges as yee shall heare afterwards.

Right soon after the decrease of Saynte Albon there came dyvers menes into England of dyvers nations, so that the good rule of Massonry was destroyed untill the tyme of Knigte Athelstone that was a woorthy King of England, and brought all this Land into rest and peace, and buyled many greate workes of abeys and Towers and many other buyldings. And he loved well Massons, and had a sonne that height Edwin, and he loved Massons muche more than his Father did, and he was a great practyser of Geometry, and he drew him muche to talke and commune with massons to learn of them the Craft, and afterwards for love that he had to Massons and to the Craft he was made a Masson. And he got of the Kyng his father a Charter and a Comission to houlde every yere Assembly once a yere where they woulde within thee Realme of England, and to correct within them faults and trespasses that were done within the Craft. And he held himselfe an Assembly at York, and there he made Massons and gave them chardges and taught them, and commanded that rule to be kept for ever after, and gave them the Charter and the Commission to keepe and made an ordynance that yt should be renewed from Kyng to Kyng. And when the Assembly was gathered togither he made a crye that all old Massons or young that had any wryting or understanding of the Chardges and the Manners, that were made before in this Land or in any other, that they should being and shewe them. And when yt was proved, there was founde some in Freanche, some in Greeke and some in English, and some in other languages, and they were all to one intent. And he made a booke thereof howe the Craft was founde, and he himselfe bade and commanded that yt should be redd or told when any Masson should be made, and for to give his Chardges.

And from that daye untill this tyme Manner of Masons have byn kept in that forme as well as men might govern yt. Furtharmore at dyvers Assemblies certain Chardges have byn made and ordeyned by the best advice of Masters and Fellowes.

Tunc unus ex senioribus tenent librum, et ille vel illi opponunt manut sub libri, et tunc precepta deberent legi &.

Every man that is a Masson take right good heed to those Charges yf that any fynde himselfe gylty in any of these Chardges that he may amend himself agaynste Gode. And especially ye that are to be chardged take good heede that ye keepe these Chardges right well for yt is great perill, a man to forsware himselfe upon a booke.

I The fyrste Chardge ys this. That ye shall be trewe men to God and holly Churche, and that yee use nor error nor heresye by your understanding or discretion, but be ye discreet men or wyse men in each thing.

II And also that ye should be leidge men to the King of England, without treason or any other falsehood, and that ye knowe no treason nor treechery but that ye amend freelyie if you maye, or else warne the Kyng or his Counsell thereof.

III And also ye shall be true eache one to another, that is to say to every Masson on the Craft of Massonry that be Massons allowed, ye shall doe unto them as ye would that they should do unto you.

IV And also that you kepe all the Counsells of your Fellowes truely, be yt in Lodge or in Chamber, and all other councells that ought to be keept by the waye of Masonhoode.

V And also that no Masson shall be a thiefe in compayne so far forth as he maye witt or knowe, and that he shall be true eache one to other, or to the Lord or Master that he serve, and truely to see to his profits and to his vantadge.

VI And also you shall call Massons your Fellowes or Brethren and none other foule names.

VII And also you shall not take your Fellowes weif in vyllany nor desyre ungodly his daughter, nor his servant, (nor) put him to no diswoorship.

VIII And also that ye pay trewly for his meate and drynke there wheare you goe to boorde.

IX And also ye shall doe no villany in that place where you goe to boorde, whereby the Crafte might be slandered.

These be the Chardges in generall that longith to every true Freemason to keepe both Masters and Fellowes.

Rehearse I will other Chardges singular for Masters and Fellowes.

(i) First that no Master or Fellowe take upon him any Lords Woorke, nor any other mans woorke unless he knowe himselfe able and sufficient of cunning to performe the same, so that their Crafte have no slander or disworshippe therby, but that the Lord maye be well and truely served.

(ii) And that no Master take no worke but that he take yt reasonable, so that the Lorde maye be well served with his owne good, and the Master to lyve honestly, and to paye his Fellowes trewly their paye as the manner is.

(iii) And also that no Master nor Fellow shall not supplant any other of their woorke, that is to saye yf he have taken a worke in hand, or els stand Master of the Lordes worke; he shall not put him out except he shall be unable of cuning to end the work.

(iv) And also that no Master or Fellowe take no prentice but for thee terme of vij yeres, and the apprentice be able of byrthe, that is to saye free born and of lymes as a man ought to be.

(v) And also that no Master nor Fellowes take no allowance to be made Masson, without Counscell of his Fellowes, and that he take him for no lesse tyme than vi or vij yeres, and that he which shall be made a Masson be able in all manner degrees, that is to saye free born, come of good kyndred, true and no bond man. And also that he have right lymes a man ought to have.

(vi) Also that no man take any prentice unless he have sufficient occupation for to sett him on, or to sett iii of his Fellowes, or ii at the least, on worke.

(vii) And also that no Master nor Fellowe shall take no mans woorke to taske that was wont to goe on journey.

(viii) Also that every Master shall give paye to his Fellowes, but as they deserve, so that he be not deceived with false workmen.

(ix) And also that noe mason slander any other behynde his back to make him lose his good name or his worldly goods.

(x) Also that no Fellow within the Lodge or without myanswer another ungodly nor reproachfully without reasonable cause.

(xi) Also that every Masson shall reverence his elder and put him to worship.

(xii) And also that no masson shall be common player at hassard or at dyce, nor at non other unlawfull playes whereby the Craft might be slandered.

(xiii) And also that no Masson shall use no leachery nor be no baude wherby the Craft might be slandered.

(xiv) And also that no Fellowe goe into the towne a nighte tymes without there is a Lodge of Fellowes, without he gave a fellow with him that he might beare him wytness that he was in honest place.

(xv) Also that every Master and Fellowe shall come to the Assembly, that if that it be within fyftie mylles about him, yf he have any warning.

(xvi) And if he have trespassed against the Crafte then he to abyde the award of the Masters and Fellowes.

(xvii) Also that every Master and Fellowe that have trespassed against the Crafte shall stand then to the award of the Masters and Fellowes, to make them accord if they can, and if they may not accorde then to goe to the comon lawe.

(xviii) Also that no Master nor Fellowe make no mould nor square, nor rule to no layr, nor sett no layar within the Lodge nor without it to hew no mould stones.

(xiv) And also that every Mason receive and cherishe Fellowes when they come over the countreyes, and to sett them a worke, if they will, as the manner is, that is to say if they have mould stones in his place, or els yee shall refreshe him with moony unto the next lodging.

(xx) And also that every Mason shall truely serve the Lorde for his paye, and every Master truly to make ane end of his worke be it taske or journey, if he have his commands, and all that he ought to have.

These Charges that we have now rehearsed unto you all, and all others that belong to Masons, ye shall keepe, so healpe you God and your halidome, and by this booke in your hands unto your power. Amen. So be it.

Scriptum Anno domini 1583 Die Decembris 25°

APPENDIX II

MASONRY DISSECTED

Masonry Dissected appeared in 1730. It contained, in addition to the exposure of the three degrees, an introduction, a vindication of the author, and starting with the third edition, a list of Lodges. Only the admission degree is given below, but those interested in the full contents may consult *The Early Masonic Catechisms* by Knoop, Jones & Hamer (see Recommended Books).

Enter'd 'Prentice's DEGREE.

Q. From whence came you? A. From the Holy Lodge of St. *John's*.

Q. What Recommendations brought you from thence? A. The Recommendations which I brought from the Right Worshipful Brothers and Fellows of the Right Worshipful and Holy Lodge of St. *John's*, from whence I came, and Greet you thrice heartily well.

Q. What do you come here to do?

A. Not to do my own proper Will,
But to subdue my Passion still;
The Rules of Masonry in hand to take,
And daily Progress therein make.

Q. Are you a Mason? A. I am so taken and Accepted to be amongst Brothers and Fellows.

Q. How shall I know that you are a Mason? A. By Signs and Tokens and perfect Points of my Entrance.

Q. What are Signs? A. All Squares, Angles and Perpendiculars.

Q. What are Tokens? A. Certain Regular and Brotherly Gripes.

Exam. Give me the Points of your Entrance. Resp. Give me

the first, and I'll give you the second.

Exam. I Hail it. Resp. I Conceal it.

Exam. What do you Conceal? Resp. All Secrets and Secresy of Masons and Masonry, unless to a True and Lawful Brother after due Examination, or in a just and worshipful Lodge of Brothers and Fellows well met.

Q. Where was you made a Mason? A. In a Just and Perfect Lodge.

Q. What makes a Just and Perfect Lodge? A. Seven or more.

Q. What do they consist of? A. One Master, two Wardens, two Fellow-Crafts and two Enter'd 'Prentices.

Q. What makes a Lodge? A. Five.

Q. What do they consist of? A. One Master, two Wardens, one Fellow-Craft, one Enter'd 'Prentice.

Q. Who brought you to the Lodge? A. An Enter'd 'Prentice.

Q. How did he bring you? A. Neither naked nor cloathed, barefoot nor shod, deprived of all Metal and in a right moving Posture.

Q. How got you Admittance? A. By three great Knocks.

Q. Who receiv'd you? A. A Junior Warden.

Q. How did he dispose of you? A. He carried me up to the North-East Part of the Lodge, and brought me back again to the West and deliver'd me to the Senior Warden.

Q. What did the Senior Warden do with you? A. He presented me, and shew'd me how to walk up (by three Steps) to the Master.

Q. What did the Master do with you? A. He made me a Mason.

Q. How did he make you a Mason? A. With my bare-bended Knee and Body within the Square, the Compass extended to my naked Left Breast, my naked Right Hand on the Holy Bible; there I took the Obligation (or Oath) of a Mason.

Q. Can you repeat that Obligation? A. I'll do my Endeavour. *(Which is as follows.)*

I Hereby solemnly Vow and Swear in the Presence of Almighty God and this Right Worshipful Assembly, that I will Hail and Conceal, and never Reveal the Secrets or Secresy of Masons or Masonry, that shall be Revealed unto me; unless to a

True and Lawful Brother, after due Examination, or in a Just and Worshipful Lodge of Brothers and Fellows well met.

I furthermore Promise and Vow, that I will not Write them, Print them, Mark them, Carve them or Engrave them, or cause them to be Written, Printed, Marked, Carved or Engraved on Wood or Stone, so as the Visible Character or Impression of a Letter may appear, whereby it may be unlawfully obtain'd.

All this under no less Penalty than to have my Throat cut, my Tongue taken from the Roof of my Mouth, my Heart pluck'd from under my Left Breast, them to be buried in the Sands of the Sea, the Length of a Cable-rope from Shore, where the Tide ebbs and flows twice in 24 Hours, my Body to be burnt to Ashes, my Ashes to be scatter'd upon the Face of the Earth, so that there shall be no more Remembrance of me among Masons.

So help me God.

Q. What Form is the Lodge? A. A Long Square.

Q. How long? A. From East to West.

Q. How broad? A. From North to South.

Q. How high? A. Inches, Feet and Yards innumerable, as high as the Heavens.

Q. How deep? A. To the Centre of the Earth.

Q. Where does the Lodge stand? A. Upon Holy Ground, or the highest Hill or lowest Vale, or in the Vale of *Jehosaphat*, or any other secret Place.

Q. How is it situated? A. Due East and West.

Q. Why so? A. Because all Churches and Chapels are or ought to be so.

Q. What supports a Lodge? A. Three great Pillars.

Q. What are they called? A. Wisdom, Strength and Beauty.

Q. Why so? A. Wisdom to contrive, Strength to support, and Beauty to adorn.

Q. What Covering have you to the Lodge? A. A clouded Canopy of divers Colours (or the Clouds.)

Q. Have you any Furniture in your Lodge? A. Yes.

Q. What is it? A. *Mosaick* Pavement, Blazing Star and Indented Tarsel.

Q. What are they? A. *Mosaick* Pavement, the Ground Floor of the Lodge, Blazing Star the Centre, and Indented Tarsel the Border round about it.

Q. What is the other Furniture of a Lodge? A. Bible, Compass and Square.

Q. Who do they properly belong to? A. Bible to God, Compass to the Master, and Square to the Fellow-Craft.

Q. Have you any Jewels in the Lodge? A. Yes.

Q. How many? A. Six. Three Moveable, and three Immoveable.

Q. What are the Moveable Jewels? A. Square, Level and Plumb-Rule.

Q. What are their Uses. A. Square to lay down True and Right Lines, Level to try all Horizontals, and the Plumb-Rule to try all Uprights.

Q. What are the Immoveable Jewels? A. Trasel Board, Rough Ashler, and Broach'd Thurnel.

Q. What are their Uses? A. Trasel Board for the Master to draw his Designs upon, Rough Ashler for the Fellow-Craft to try their Jewels upon, and the Broach'd Thurnel for the Enter'd 'Prentice to learn to work upon.

Q. Have you any Lights in your Lodge? A. Yes, Three.

Q. What do they represent? A. Sun, Moon and Master-Mason.

N.B. *These Lights are three large Candles placed on high Candlesticks.*

Q. Why so? A. Sun to rule the Day, Moon the Night, and Master-Mason his Lodge.

Q. Have you any fix'd Lights in your Lodge: A. Yes.

Q. How many? A. Three.

N.B. *These fix'd Lights are Three Windows, suppos'd (tho' vainly) to be in every Room where a Lodge is held, but more properly the four Cardinal Points according to the antique Rules of Masonry.*

Q. How are they situated? A. East, South and West.

Q. What are their Uses? A. To light the Men to, at and from their Work.

Q. Why are there no Lights in the North? A. Because the Sun darts no Rays from thence.

Q. Where stands your Master? A. In the East.

Q. Why so? A. As the Sun rises in the East and opens the Day, so the Master stands in the East [*with his Right Hand upon his Left Breast being a Sign, and the Square about his Neck*] to open the Lodge and to set his men at Work.

Q. Where stands your Wardens? A. In the West.

Q. What's their Business? A. As the Sun sets in the West to close the Day, so the Wardens stand in the West [*with their Right Hands upon their Left Breasts being a Sign, and the Level and Plumb-Rule about their Necks*] to close the Lodge and dismiss the Men from Labour, paying their Wages.

Q. Where stands the Senior Enter'd 'Prentice? A. In the South.

Q. What is his Business? A. To hear and receive instructions and welcome strange Brothers.

Q. Where stands the Junior Enter'd 'Prentice? A. In the North.

Q. What is his Business? A. To keep off all Cowans and Evesdroppers.

Q. If a Cowan (or Listner) is catch'd, how is he to be punished? A. To be plac'd under the Eves of the Houses (in rainy Weather) till the Water runs in at his Shoulders and out at his Shoos.

Q. What are the Secrets of a Mason? A. Signs, Tokens and many Words.

Q. Where do you keep those Secrets? A. Under my Left Breast.

Q. Have you any Key to those Secrets? A. Yes.

Q. Where do you keep it? A. In a Bone Bone Box that neither opens nor shuts but with Ivory Keys.

Q. Does it hang or does it lie? A. It hangs.

Q. What does it hang by? A. A Tow-Line 9 Inches or a Span.

Q. What Metal is it of? A. No manner of Metal at all; but a Tongue of good Report is as good behind a Brother's Back as before his Face.

N.B. *The Key is the Tongue, the Bone Bone Box the Teeth, the Tow-Line the Roof of the Mouth.*

Q. How many Principles are there in Masonry? A. Four.

Q. What are they? A. Point, Line, Superficies and Solid.

Q. Explain them. A. Point the Centre *(round which the Master cannot err)* Line Length without Breadth, Superficies Length and Breadth, Solid comprehends the whole.

Q. How many Principle-Signs? A. Four.

Q. What are they? A. Guttural, Pectoral, Manual and Pedestal.

Q. Explain them. A. Guttural the Throat, Pectoral the Breast, Manual the Hand, Pedestal the Feet.

Q. What do you learn by being a Gentleman-Mason. A. Secresy, Morality and Goodfellowship.

Q. What do you learn by being an Operative Mason? A. Hue, Square, Mould-stone, lay a Level and raise a Perpendicular.

Q. Have you seen your Master to-day? A. Yes.

Q. How was he Cloathed? A. In a Yellow Jacket and Blue Pair of Breeches.

N.B. *The Yellow Jacket is the Compasses, and the Blue Breeches the Steel Points.*

Q. How long do you serve your Master? A. From Monday Morning to Saturday Night.

Q. How do you serve him? A. With Chalk, Charcoal and Earthen Pan.

Q. What do they denote? A. Freedom, Fervency and Zeal.

Ex. Give me the Entre'd 'Prentice's Sign. Resp. Extending the Four Fingers of the Right Hand and drawing of them cross his Throat, is the Sign, and demands a Token.

N.B. *A Token is by joining the Ball of the Thumb of the Right Hand upon the first Knuckle of the Fore-finger of the Brother's Right Hand that demands a Word.*

Q. Give me the Word. A. I'll letter it with You.

Exam. BOAZ. [N.B. *The Exam. says* B, *Resp.* O, *Exam.* A, *Resp.* Z, i.e. Boaz.] Give me another.

Resp. JACHIN. [N.B. Boaz *and* Jachin *were two Pillars in* Solomon's *Porch.* 1 Kings, chap. vii. ver. 21.]

Q. How old are you? A. Under Seven. [*Denoting he has not pass'd Master*]

Q. What's the Day for? A. To See in.

Q. What's the Night for? A. To Hear.

Q. How blows the Wind? A. Due East and West.

Q. What's a Clock? A. High Twelve.

The End of the Enter'd 'Prentice's Part.

APPENDIX III

THE CHARGE TO THE INITIATE TAKEN FROM WILLIAM SMITH'S POCKET COMPANION, 1735

This clear and comprehensive statement of Masonic ideals made its first appearance in print in 1735 in *William Smith's Pocket Companion*. The latter was based on the first edition of Anderson's *Constitutions*, but contained in addition, a Charge to the Initiate. Although the words differ from the Charge we know today, fundamentally it corresponds very closely:

A SHORT

CHARGE

To be given to new admitted

BRETHREN.

You are now admitted, by the unanimous Consent of our Lodge, a Fellow of our most Antient and Honourable Society; Antient, as having subsisted from times immemorial, and Honourable, as tending in every Particular to render a Man so, that will be but conformable to its glorious Precepts. The greatest Monarchs in all Ages, as well of Asia and Africa as of Europe, have been Encouragers of the Royal Art; and many of them have presided as Grand Masters over the Masons in their respective Territories, not thinking it any lessening to their Imperial Dignities to level themselves with their Brethren in Masonry, and to act as they did.

The Word's great Architect is our Supreme Master, and the unerring Rule, he has given us, is that by which we work.

Religious Disputes are never suffered in the Lodge; for as Masons, we only pursue the universal Religion or the Religion of Nature. This is the Cement which unites Men of the most different Principles in one sacred Band, and brings together those which were the most distant from one another.

There are three general Heads of Duty which Masons ought always to inculcate, viz., to God, our Neighbours, and Ourselves.

To God, in never mentioning his Name but with that Reverential Awe which becomes a Creature to bear to his Creator, and to look upon him always as the Summum Bonum which we came into the World to enjoy; and according to that View to regulate all our Pursuits.

To our Neighbours, in acting upon the Square, or doing as we would be done by.

To Ourselves, in avoiding all Intemperances and Excesses, whereby we may be rendered incapable of following our Work, or led into Behaviour unbecoming our laudable Profession, and in always keeping within due Bounds, and free from all Pollution.

In the State, a Mason is to behave as a peacable and dutiful Subject, conforming cheerfully to the Government under which he lives.

He is to pay a due Deference to his Superiors, and from his Inferiors he is rather to receive Honour with some Reluctance, than to extort it.

He is to be a Man of Benevolence and Charity, not sitting down contented while his Fellow Creatures, but much more his Brethren, are in Want, when it is in his Power (without prejudicing himself or Family) to relieve them.

In the Lodge, he is to behave with all due Decorum, lest the Beauty and Harmony thereof should be disturbed or broke.

He is to be obedient to the Master and presiding Officers, and to apply himself closely to the Business of Masonry, that he may sooner become a Proficient therein, both for his own Credit, and for that of the Lodge.

He is not to neglect his own necessary Avocations for the sake of Masonry, nor to involve himself in Quarrels with those who through Ignorance may speak evil of, or ridicule it.

He is to be a Lover of Arts and Sciences, and to take all Opportunities of improving himself therein.

If he recommends a Friend to be made a Mason, he must vouch him to be such as he really believes will conform to the aforesaid Duties, lest by his Misconduct at any time the Lodge should pass under some evil Imputations. Nothing can prove more shocking to all faithful Masons, than to see any of their Brethren profane or break through the Sacred Rules of their Order, and such as can do it they wish had never been admitted.

APPENDIX IV

THE CHARGE TO THE INITIATE TAKEN FROM WM. PRESTON'S ILLUSTRATIONS OF MASONRY *1772*

Another version of the Charge to the Initiate is to be found in William Preston's *Illustrations of Masonry*, published in 1772. In the Appendix of that publication appeared:

> A Charge on Masonry. To be delivered after the ceremony of Initiation into the First Degree.

The first edition of the *Illustrations* contain a recommendation by Grand Lodge Officers including the Grand Master, stating:

> We having perused the said Book, and finding it to correspond with the ancient practices of this society, do recommend the same.

The Grand Lodge which thus endorsed the *Illustrations* was the premier Grand Lodge, or the so-called Moderns.

The Antients Grand Lodge favoured the Charge given in Smith's *Pocket Companion*, for in 1800, the fifth edition of *Ahiman Rezon*, the Book of Constitutions of the Antients, contained a Charge very similar to that in Smith's book.

Entitled 'A Short Charge to a New-admitted Mason', it added to the latter the following paragraph:

> From the attention you have paid to the recital of this Charge, we are led to hope that you will estimate the real value of Free-Masonry, and imprint on your mind those dictates of truth, honour, and justice, which it so forcibly enjoins.

A CHARGE
on
MASONRY

To be delivered after the ceremony of Initiation into the First Degree'.
Taken from Wm. Preston's Illustrations of Masonry *of 1772.*

Brother, As I have had the honour to introduce you into the first principles of our Royal Order, I have now the pleasure to congratulate you on being accepted a Member of this most ancient and honourable Society: ancient, as having subsisted from time immemorial; and honourable, as tending, in every particular, to render all men so, who will be but conformable to its glorious precepts. No society ever subsisted which was raised on a better principle or more solid foundation; nor were ever more excellent rules and useful maxims laid down, than are inculcated on all persons when initiated into the mysteries of this science. Monarchs, in all ages, have been encouragers and promoters of this Art, and have never deemed it derogatory from their dignity to level themselves with the fraternity, to extend their privileges, and to patronize their assemblies.

As a gentleman and a Mason you are bound to be a strict observer of the moral law, as contained in this holy book; to consider it as the unerring standard of truth and justice, and to regulate your life and actions by its divine precepts. Herein your duty to God, to your neighbour, and to yourself, is duly inculcated; and, as a zealous attachment to these duties will secure both public and private esteem, I hope your future conduct will amply evince the happy effects of this fraternal admonition.

In the state, you are to be a quiet and peaceable subject, true to your sovereign, and just to your country; never to countenance disloyalty or rebellion, but patiently to submit to magisterial authority, and conform with cheerfulness to the government of the kingdom in which you live.

In your outward demeanour, you are to be particularly careful to avoid censure or reproach; and to beware of all those who may artfully endeavour to insinuate themselves into your esteem, with a view to betray your virtuous resolutions, or make you swerve from the honourable principles of this institution. Let not interest, favour, or prejudice, ever bias your integrity, or influence you to be guilty of a dishonourable action; but let the whole series of your conduct and behaviour be regular and uniform, and your deportment suitable to the dignity of this laudable profession.

Above all other virtues, practise benevolence and charity; two of the most distinguishing characteristics of this venerable institution. The inconceivable pleasure of contributing towards the relief of our fellow-creatures can only be experienced by persons of a humane disposition; who are naturally excited, by the power of sympathy, to extend their aid in alleviation of the miseries of others. This alone encourages the generous soul to distribute his bounty with cheerfulness. By supporting himself in their unhappy situation, he listens to their complaints with attention, bewails their misfortunes, and speedily relieves their distress.

The next object of your attention, and which more immediately relates to your present state, is our excellent *Book of Constitutions*; containing the history of the Craft from the earliest periods, and an entertaining detail of those noble personages who have enriched the Art from Adam to the present era; with all the laws and regulations of the society, necessary for the instruction of the fraternity; and to which, I hope, you will ever conform and adhere.

A punctual attendance on our assemblies I would next enjoin, more especially on the duties of this Lodge. Here, as in all other regular meetings of the fraternity, you are to behave with due order and decorum, that harmony may be preserved, and the business of the society be properly conducted. You are not to lay, or offer to lay, wagers; nor use any unbecoming language in derogation of the name of God, or towards the corruption of good manners; neither are you to introduce, support, or maintain yourself ludicrously while the Lodge is engaged in what is serious and important; but to pay a proper deference and respect to the Master and presiding officers, and diligently to apply to your work in Masonry, that you may the sooner become a proficient therein, as well for your own reputation, as the honor of the Lodge in which you have been made.

However, although I would earnestly solicit your frequent appearance at our regular meetings, yet I mean not to interfere with your necessary avocations; for these are on no occasion to be neglected. At your leisure hours you are required to study only the liberal arts and sciences; and, by that means, with a few private instructions, you will soon attain a competent knowledge of our Masonic mysteries.

Before I conclude, I must recall to your memory the absolute necessity of keeping inviolable every particular instruction of this solemn charge; and that if ever, in the circle of your acquaintance, you should find one desirous of being accepted among Masons, you will be particularly attentive not to recommend him, unless you are convinced he will conform to these rules; in order that the honour, glory, and reputation of this noble institution may be firmly established, and the popular world be fully convinced of its benign influence.

Thus, Brother, I have recapitulated those duties I could wish you carefully to observe; and hope, from the apparent attention you have paid to their recital, that you will estimate their real value, and ever imprint on your mind the sacred dictates of truth, honour, and justice.

INDEX